101 more
Business Letters

1/04

Edited by

David Crosby

Wyvern Crest
Publications

Published by

Wyvern Crest Publications
A Division of
Wyvern Crest Limited
Wyvern House
6 The Business Park
Ely
Cambs
CB7 4JW
01353 665522

First published in 1997

© Wyvern Crest Limited 1997

British Library Cataloguing in Publication Data
A catalogue record for this book is available from the British Library

ISBN 1 899206 09 4

Text design by Lisa Alderson
Typeset by Pantek Arts, Maidstone, Kent.
Printed by Bell and Bain Limited, Glasgow.

101 *more* Business Letters

Rattle out business letters in a fraction of the time

It is difficult to compose, write and sign a business letter in under 20 minutes. Many letters, if you think about it, can take 30 or 40 minutes, or even an hour each, just to get sorted. The morning post can be the start of a frustrating, time-consuming irritation for many managers.

It doesn't have to be that way. All the letters in this book may be copied straight from the page, and some will require only a slight amendment. With other letters, you may want to take a phrase here or a paragraph there and slot it into the rest of your letter. The important thing to remember is that the 'thinking' has already been done for you - so, those difficult situations, where you can't quite get the right words together, can now be banished ... forever.

Your time is expensive - this book could save you £££s

When a typical letter can cost a business about £15 to send out, mostly in the time of the manager composing it, anything that can bring this cost down will make a big difference. With over 100 letters in this guide (each costing a fraction of this amount), it is easy to see how many pounds you can save by slicing hours off your letter writing time.

Angry letters, friendly letters, diplomatic letters, letters that get results

Identifying how subtle tones in a letter are achieved using different phrases is not always easy to pinpoint. What makes, for example, the tone in a letter of complaint either friendly, neutral, angry, diplomatic or strong? To help you find the answer, each letter in this book comes with its own incisive commentary, many of which highlight the specific words and phrases that alter the tone. The commentaries also clarify the meaning that is implicit in the words chosen, and demonstrate how a recipient will perceive and interpret those phrases, helping you to get exactly what you want.

Finding the letter you want is easy

The guide has an utterly comprehensive Contents page, which groups the letters by topic (*Employing People, Sales and Marketing Management, Debt collection* etc.). Each topic is then subdivided into further categories, for example, under *Employing People* you will find (amongst others) *Interviews and offers, References, Motivating staff, Offering sincere condolences* etc. Each letter is also numbered for ease of reference.

But what if you want to look up all the letters concerned with say, negotiating? All you have to do is turn to the *Index of letters by type* on page xiii, where a comprehensive list of these letters (and other types) will be found. For a final catch-all, there is a comprehensive topic index at the end of the work.

Copyright

No matter what letter you have to write, *101 more Business Letters* offers countless ways of phrasing business letters. Use it regularly and it will amply repay you, not only in time saved, but also in helping you to clinch deals, get debts paid quickly, obtain better prices and persuade people to your way of thinking. Whatever the letter, I wish you every success.

More time-saving letters

101 more Business Letters is a companion book to *101 Business Letters*. If you don't have both books, don't worry - each one can be used on its own. Of course, if you do have both of them you will have access to a more comprehensive range of letters and a greater variety of situations and lessons to be learned. Here are just some of the letters and topics in *101 Business Letters* not covered in this work:

- Dealing with advertising agencies
- Handling a customer who is trying it on
- Insurance
- Firing a strong warning shot at a supplier
- International trade
- Demanding that defective work be made good
- Rejecting an invitation to 'contra' invoices
- Announcing court proceedings in seven days
- Notifying a buyer about a discount for prompt payment
- Notifying an employee of her entitlement to maternity pay
- Resigning from a job
- Negotiating a request for more commission
- Written warnings before dismissal
- Dismissing an agent for working for a competitor
- Health and safety issues

While the letters in both *101 Business Letters* and *101 more Business Letters* are different, we have kept the appendixes and introduction in each volume the same. The appendixes will be one of the most sought after sections (by your colleagues as well as yourself) and we feel it is important to make this information accessible in each volume. So, if a colleague happens to 'borrow' one of the volumes, you won't be left high and dry! Unless, of course, *both* volumes have been 'borrowed', in which case I recommend you buy another set!

David Crosby
January 1997

CONTENTS

CHAPTER 2 Managing Customers

CHAPTER 3 Debt Collection and Credit Control

CHAPTER 4 Employing People

CHAPTER 5 Sales and Marketing Management

CHAPTER 6 Banking and Property

CHAPTER 7 Business and the Community

INDEX OF LETTERS BY TYPE

This index is designed to be used with the contents and the main index at the end of the work. The Contents gives a good overview of the letters concerned with suppliers, customers, employees and so on. But, if you have to write a complaining letter (and want to compare these kinds of letters that are spread throughout the work), it is difficult to find them easily by examining the Contents. However, if you look up *Complaining* in this index you will find a list of the letters featured, that are concerned with this topic.

Acknowledgements

The Publisher would like to thank the customers who contributed letters to this guide, including: David Lambert of APTECH, Peter Le Conte of Van der Windt Packaging (UK) Ltd, DR Radia of NRG Victory Reinsurance Ltd, Eddie Mander of GCS, DRE Clark of the AEC Group of Companies Ltd and Martin Oates of BSG Products. Special thanks also to Vic Blake of Cambridge for his contributions to the work.

CHAPTER ONE

Managing Suppliers

Suppliers often need to be held on a tight rein. Whether you need to query a quotation, place an order, negotiate a special arrangement, or simply want to make a complaint using a stern reproach, this chapter offers ideas and solutions designed to keep your suppliers firmly under your control. Just a few of the highlights are featured here.

Need to negotiate a better price?
Suppliers may sometimes be tempted to nudge their prices up above the competition. If you want to keep them on their toes, try letter 2 to negotiate a keen quotation.

Need to sell a new idea to a supplier?
Sometimes you may need to change the way you want suppliers to do things for you. If a supplier has been doing it in a certain way for you for a long time you will need to sell the idea and persuade them to accept that you want it done differently. Letter 10 shows how to bring them around to your way of thinking.

Stand up to unreasonable terms and conditions
Don't let a supplier get away with unreasonable terms and conditions. And don't fall into the trap of thinking they won't try to enforce them. Sort them out when placing your order and stand up for your rights. Remember, you are the customer. Letter 5 illustrates it in practice.

Making a stern reproach
When complaining, make sure that you strike the right note to produce the desired response. Too harsh, and you risk alienating your suppliers. Too soft, and they may walk all over you. Seven different letters portray some of the options available to you.

The supplier here has a good existing relationship with the customer. There is no need to specify delivery instructions as the supplier knows where the parts are to be sent. The specification, though, remains clearly set out.

It is good idea to give the date by when you want the quote – this helps bring it to the top of the supplier's priorities. If he then gives you the quote after the date requested, you will be able to come down harder on him. Otherwise, you could be greeted with excuses such as 'I didn't realise it was so urgent'.

Fenner & Sons

16 George Street, Woodbridge,
Suffolk IP3 7KL
Tel: (01394) 198423
Fax: (01394) 198444
Registered in England: 91221299
VAT No: 919129075 80

Mr J M Hibberd
Sales Manager
Pecklacks (Metals) Ltd
Drovers Lane
Slough
SL42 3RG

31 May 1999

Dear Jim

I am delighted to say that our sales are ahead of expectations and so we are boosting our production. Consequently, we need more parts urgently (within ten days of placing the order). The parts are:

Item:	Part No:	Unit:	Quantity:
1.5" Aluminium Trunking	B14375	3 metre	10
Lock Nuts	J388851	each	60
2" Mild Steel Bolts	J388232	each	60
Closing Strip	B13650	3 metre	10
Steel Brackets	C18724	each	27
Steel Brackets	C18725	each	3

We shall be making our decision on Thursday 12 June, so please let me have your prices by that date.

Yours sincerely

Patrick Thompson
Production Manager

SIMPSON & MARTIN

39 TOP STREET
STOKE-ON-TRENT
ST2 3DR UNITED KINGDOM
Tel: (01782) 156232 Fax: (01782) 120899
Reg. No: England 96223978 VAT No: 91210674

Mr T Edwards
Sales Director
Bond & Bond Paper Merchants
12-16 Little Lane
Great Langdale
Ambleside
Cumbria
CU2 7BT

6 Oct 1999

Dear Tony,

Your quotation no. TE/219785
Thanks for your quotation for supplying 30 reams of 85gsm paper. I am aware the price of paper has been escalating recently but, frankly, I am not at all happy with this price or your suggestion for remedying the situation.

We had an explicit agreement that your prices would remain unchanged until the end of the calendar year. I took this to mean that all goods *ordered* before the end of the calendar year would be supplied at that year's rate. The fact that the order cannot be supplied until the new year is, frankly, not our problem.

Incidentally, I have received a quotation from a direct competitor of yours at Make-it Paper who has offered to guarantee your *original* price for the next six months.

In the light of this, may I suggest that you reconsider your quotation to us. If you are unable to match Make-it Paper's price, then I regret that we shall have no option but to transfer our business.

Yours sincerely

Mike Moy
Senior Buyer

Where a customer has an existing agreement with a supplier and the supplier has chosen to forget or ignore a substantive term, a stern letter is called for. This one has the backing of the agreement which has been broken and the negotiating power that a better price can be obtained elsewhere.

The supplier has no options but to back down or face losing the business. If the customer had not obtained a more competitive quote, then the last sentence, which threatens to transfer the business, should be omitted. It wouldn't carry the same weight and a supplier may take it for what it would be – just an idle threat.

The service here is critical to the buyer. She needs the disk back urgently and is placing the order on the understanding it will be returned on a specified day. Note how she doesn't simply say she is enclosing a cheque but breaks down the charge into its various components showing how the amount is arrived at. The implication in this letter is 'if anything is different from what is specified here, I expect you to let me know'.

SIMPSON & MARTIN

39 TOP STREET
STOKE-ON-TRENT
ST2 3DR UNITED KINGDOM
Tel: (01782) 156232 Fax: (01782) 120899
Reg. No: England 96223978 VAT No: 91210674

Ms Jenny Croft
Sales Co-ordinator
CJB Services
Highfield House
Standish Industrial Estate
Wigan
WN7 9OE

23 February 1999

Dear Jenny,

Disk Conversion
Following our telephone conversation today, I enclose a copy of the Apple Mac Disk (Word 3.0) which I would like converted to Word for Windows 3.1.

I understand the charge for this is £10 + £20 for the express service + VAT. I therefore have pleasure in enclosing a cheque for £35.25.

I understand the express service means you will send the disk back the same day it is received by 1st class post. On this basis, I look forward to receiving the disk back on Friday 25 February.

As we shall be needing this service again, I would be grateful if you could arrange for an account to be opened.

Yours sincerely

Nina Rose
Publications Assistant

⊛ WILSON SMITH LTD

A wholly-owned subsidiary of The Wilson Group PLC
16 Willow Walk, Retford, Nottingham NG6 8WS
Tel: (01777) 121211 Fax: (01777) 121233
Reg. No: England 1212298762

Facsimile Message

To:	RPP Holdings plc
F.A.O.:	Bob Taylor
From:	Tom Greate
Date:	23 August 1999
No. of Pages:	1

Dear Bob

Wilson Smith Quality Manual
Oops! We've made a real clanger.

Don has just created a sample of the contents for our quality manual, which he has inserted into the ringbinder – only to discover that the binder is too small. It seems that someone here interpreted the extent of 350 *leaves* as 350 *pages*.

Is it too late to change the order? I tried to call you but your phone was continuously engaged, so I am faxing this to you instead.

Please call me back urgently so we can discuss this.

Yours sincerely

Tom Greate
Quality Manager

If you do make a mistake, it is best to sort it out as soon as possible. This letter would be written to a supplier who is well known to you.

The unconventional opening contains an element of surprise, signifying that it is not just a piece of routine correspondence, but something that demands immediate attention. The friendly tone also sets the scene for the supplier to forgive you for overlooking something so simple and, importantly, tells them immediately that it is not his fault.

When you start trading with a new company, it is important to check on and agree the terms and conditions of supply. It is no use the supplier sending his quotation, listing his terms and conditions of supply, and then you sending your purchase order with its terms and conditions of purchase, and hoping that will do. What happens later on if there is a dispute? It is far better to clarify at the outset conflicting terms.

One of the commonest areas that is open to misinterpretation is what is meant by 30 days' credit. Is it literally 30 days from the date of the invoice? Or is the interpretation that the buying company makes here correct? Make sure you are clear about what is meant.

There are two phrases to note here: "...subject to...", which is very useful when you want to qualify a particular term and "...we reserve the right to...", which is handy when you want the option, but not the obligation, to do something.

IDENDEN INDUSTRIES
A division of Idenden Plc
Porter House, Hull HU7 4RF England

Tel 01482 119087 Fax 01482 119088
Registered in England No: 1218943

Mr G Glover
Sales Manager
Christian Engineering
Rochdale Road
Middleton
Manchester
M24 5TH

14 July 1999

Dear Gordon,

PURCHASE ORDER NO. 298745
Here is our purchase order no. 298745 for the boxes. Please let your accounts people know that they must quote this purchase order number on all invoices and correspondence, otherwise payment will be delayed.

Please also note the following points regarding the terms and conditions:

Clause 4 Terms
Your payment terms of 30 days are subject to the timing of our payment runs. We settle all invoices at the end of the month in which they fall due for payment. An invoice dated 25th August, for example, will be paid on 30th September, as will an invoice dated 5th August. Accordingly, we cannot accept your interest on overdue accounts as some may appear to be overdue when they are not.

Clause 13 Quantity
We are not prepared to pay a premium to ensure delivery of the exact order quantity so we must accept that there may be some slight variation. However, we reserve the right to return over deliveries rather than pay for them, if they are not needed.

Clause 19 Intellectual Property
I do not accept this clause as written. Any copyright you own, you will continue to own. Any copyright we own, we will continue to own. Your work on our behalf does not entitle you to copyright on anything we have designed.

Clause 21 Title & Risk in the goods.
We do not accept clause (b). It is your responsibility to ensure safe delivery of the goods to us. We will not become liable to pay for any goods that do not reach us in satisfactory condition.

Finally, I enclose the customer credit application form duly completed and signed. It is subject to the contents of this letter.

Yours sincerely

Michael Preston
Marketing Manager

⊛ **WILSON SMITH LTD**

A wholly-owned subsidiary of The Wilson Group PLC
16 Willow Walk, Retford, Nottingham NG6 8WS
Tel: (01777) 121211 Fax: (01777) 121233
Reg. No: England 1212298762

Mr Trevor Goodge
Sales Manager
Idenden Industries
Porter House
Hull
HU7 4RF

15 June 1999

Dear Trevor,

Your invoice no. 85903

I have received in the post this morning your invoice no. 85903 for £300.80 for 40 high pressure seal rings.

We have no record of placing this order and your invoice omits to provide a reference. All our orders must be made on a valid purchase order and signed by an authorised signatory. I have checked with my colleagues to see if anyone has ordered these items and accidentally omitted to draft a purchase order but no one recalls placing such an order.

Before we return the goods to you, please could you let me know what reference you have for this order and I will look into the matter further for you.

Yours sincerely

Jim Bone
Purchasing Manager

Occasionally the wrong goods may be sent to the wrong company – or someone has circumvented normal procedures when buying them. Although the goods probably aren't intended for your company, it is best to check first with the supplier, just in case. Asking for the supplier's reference should help get to the bottom of the story. It would be more embarrassing to return the goods, only to find that someone high up had placed the order but not told anyone! Discretion is the better part of valour.

Note the tone used to handle the unexpected charge here. The letter offers no thanks to the company for sending the invoice but uses the more neutral "I have received..." This forewarns the reader that all may not be well.

The second paragraph has a more demonstrative tone, with useful emphatic expressions such as: "No mention was made..." and the firm "...referred expressly to the fact...". Remember, if you use the term 'expressly' the point must have been definitely stated (preferably in writing) and not implied.

Charles Cunningham Ltd
29 Baker Street, LONDON N34 6GH England
Tel: (0171) 015 1290 Fax: (0171) 015 1271
Reg. No: England 1104398135 VAT No: 82108643

Adams Office Supplies
Brentwood Road
Fulham
London
SW6 8JM

22 March 1999

Dear Sir / Madam

Your invoice number DL67501
I have received your invoice for the departmental shredder which was ordered.   I note that the invoice amount includes a delivery charge of £25.50.

When we placed our order, no mention was made by your sales representative of this charge and our Purchase Order No. WR15498 referred expressly to the fact that delivery was to be included within the price quoted. This was not queried prior to receipt of the shredder.

I look forward to receiving a credit note for the full amount of £25.50.

Yours faithfully

Joan Smith
Office Manager

Grange & Turner Ltd

32 WESTBOURN ROAD, WITNEY, OXON OX6 7HY

Telephone (01993) 107888
Fax (01993) 107843

Reg. No: England 13078453
VAT No: 75698764

Mr E Thomas
Sales Administator
Starbright Office Supplies
Wilmslow Road
Didcot
Oxon
OX7 5GH

20 March 1999

Dear Mr Thomas

Fax machines

I have received your catalogue of fax machines. Before I decide
which model to purchase, please could you advise me about the
facilities for the Sharp UX3500 and Panasonic UF321 machines:

1. What is the automatic feed capacity of each machine?

2. Will both machines accept A3 size paper?

3. What is the print resolution of the Sharp model?

4. When the catalogue refers to transmission speed in seconds,
    is this the speed it takes for one A4 sheet of paper to be
    transmitted?

Yours sincerely

John Sand
Office Manager

Product catalogues are not always clear and often omit information that a customer wants. In this letter, the potential customer has four pieces of information that he needs to know before making a decision to buy.

When faced with a number of questions, setting them out as a numbered list helps the reader to assimilate quickly what information is being asked for. The writer could just as easily have presented the items as bullet points, but it is easier for a respondent to refer to a number in a reply (especially in long lists) than to have to explain which point is being talked about.

Terms and conditions of supply should regularly be reviewed by companies. Sometimes they will need to be amended; if they do, a letter like this will be sufficient. Don't forget to include the date from when the new terms apply.

If the change is more significant than the one shown here – for example, changing payment terms to 60 days' from 30 days' – you should get written confirmation from the supplier that he agrees to the change, to avoid subsequent disputes. This could be done by asking him to countersign an enclosed copy of the letter and return it to you.

GKT Products Ltd, Unit 10, Castleway Lane, Alloway, Ayr, KA7 4BE
Telephone (01292) 177900 Fax (01292) 199855   Reg. No: 17964583 VAT No: 679845

The Sales Manager
SLP Engineering
27 Vine Street
Penrith
Cumbria
CA9 3FV

3 June 1999

Dear Sir / Madam

Amendment to terms and conditions
I am writing to advise you of a change in our terms and conditions, which affects all orders placed with us from 1 July.

All delivery notes accompanying goods supplied to us must contain the correct purchase order number. This will enable us to match up the relevant paperwork more quickly and prevent any delays in payment to you.

Thank you for your cooperation in this matter.

Yours faithfully

Jean Hardcastle
Accounts Manager

B & R HENDERSONS LTD

Marlows Road, Aberdeen AB20 5GT
Tel: 01224 267855 Fax: 01224 267977
Reg. No: 16497811 VAT No: 7387945

Robert Noyes
Sales Manager
NPB Manufacturing Ltd
4 Manor Close
Warrington
WA3 3HY

20 August 1999

Dear Robert,

Re: Progress Sheets
Thank you for your recent faxes, and I apologise for the delay in replying.

First of all, I would like to reassure you that our policy of demanding progress sheets, properly signed and dated, is designed to protect both you and other suppliers involved in the manufacturing process. With this system in place, if a problem arises at any stage in the process we will have a better idea of where the fault might lie. It also aims to catch any hitches at the start of the process, rather than on the day that our goods are meant to be delivered. All we are doing is formalising the procedure that we have always asked our subcontractors and printers to follow (see our letter 24.06.99) but that, in practice, has not been carried out.

It is not intended to be a sword hanging over anyone's head – it should be little more than an extension of what your current practices are. All our suppliers have been asked to comply with this new policy, since everyone has experienced problems in the past.

I hope this explains our reason for implementing the system satisfactorily and trust that you will be able to co-operate with its operation. Should you be uncertain about any aspect of it, please do not hesitate to give us a call.

Yours sincerely

Roger McIntyre
Manager

A supplier is questioning a new procedure that has been forced upon him. Here the supplier's customer is persuading the supplier to accept the change of policy. Note how it is being 'sold' to the supplier, not as something new but as something which he should have been doing anyway: "...it should be little more than an extension of what your current practices are...". This is a neat argument, against which there is little defence.

Declining a supplier politely is not always easy. This letter strikes an agreeable but firm tone. The politeness of the decline is helped by going for the understatement: "...it does not fit comfortably..." which contrasts with the firmer "Thanks but no thanks", which is refreshingly frank and leaves no doubt about the decision, so nobody's time is wasted.

What goes unsaid is often as important as what is said. Note how the customer does not offer any hope for the future – a clear sign that the products the supplier produces are unsuitable for this market.

Grange & Turner Ltd

32 WESTBOURN ROAD, WITNEY, OXON OX6 7HY

Telephone (01993) 107888
Fax (01993) 107843

Reg. No: England 13078453
VAT No: 75698764

Mr A French
Sales Administator
Squeeky Kleen
45 Todd Square
Glasgow
G20 5XA

28 September 1999

Dear Mr French

<u>Squeeky-kleen</u>
Thank you for your letter of 11th September and for the samples of your innovative cleaning product.

At the moment, it does not fit comfortably with our catalogue plans for the next six months and I am afraid I must say "Thanks but no thanks".

If you are thinking of doing any direct mail of your own on the product, we do have a strong mailing list of corporate customers who have bought related items. If you are interested in renting these, do give me a call.

Yours sincerely

Brian Reed
Marketing Manager

IDENDEN INDUSTRIES
A division of Idenden Plc
Porter House, Hull HU7 4RF England

Tel 01482 119087 Fax 01482 119088
Registered in England No: 1218943

Ms Elizabeth Taylor
Sales Co-ordinator
Litson & Fulton Ltd
Unit 8 Clifton Ind. Est
Clifton Road
Liverpool
L9 6DD

24 October 1999

Dear Elizabeth,

Our order no. YTL8906
I have received a consignment of sixty 30mm clips for high velocity piping in response to our order no. YTL8906. Your invoice reference no. is LP1018 dated 20 October.

My order clearly specified thirty 60 mm clips. As I have no requirement for 30mm clips in the foreseeable future I am returning these to you in a separate consignment. Please could you arrange for the 60mm clips to be despatched as soon as possible.

Thank you for your attention to this matter.

Yours sincerely

Stuart O'Neil
Purchasing Manager

Which style should be used in letters: 'I' or 'we'?

If you are writing on behalf of your company and you want the letter to sound as if it has the full weight of your organisation behind you, opt for 'we' and 'our'. If you are writing in your own right then 'I' and 'my' is preferable.

In practice there is very little to choose between the two styles although 'we' and 'our' can, in some situations, sound a touch formal. It may also be that the person writing doesn't want to take personal responsibility for what is being said in the letter.

This letter aims to present a complaint under the guise of good humour. Its tone opts for a mid-way between the formal and very casual. It succeeds in building a rapport with the reader, which will make him want to come back and put the window right.

Helen Meeting is unconcerned exactly when it will be done because she knows she can rely on John Fuller to fix the problem. The letter suggests a trust between the two which more formal business letters don't imply.

RPP Holdings Plc
35/38 New Road, Paignton, Devon TQ3 4UU
Tel: 01803 175653 Fax: 01803 187908
Reg. No: England 1976143

John Fuller
Works Manager
RG Fuller & Sons
53 Jackson Way
Tiverton
Devon
TV7 4HG

1 October 1999

Dear John

Thanks for coming to put the additional window in our office. It has really helped to lighten up the room. However, there is one minor point I want to raise with you.

For some reason, the part of the window that opens doesn't seem to want to stay in its correct position and has shuffled itself along, so that one side is scraping against the frame while the other side has an unusually large gap. Fine for a bit of ventilation in the summer months but not so pleasant when we have a howling gale!

Could you call round some time next week to have a look at it and encourage it back to its proper position? Give me a call to let me know when you are coming.

Yours sincerely

Helen Meeting
Office Manager

RPP Holdings Plc
35/38 New Road, Paignton, Devon TQ3 4UU
Tel: 01803 175653 Fax: 01803 187908
Reg. No: England 1976143

Jane Summers
Marketing Executive
Corrugated Card & Packaging Ltd
Unit 8
London Road Ind. Est.
Truro
Cornwall
TR9 7KM

12 December 1999

Dear Jane

Purchase order number 548792
We received your delivery of 500 cardboard boxes yesterday.

When our Warehouse Manager checked the number of boxes that had been supplied, he discovered that 49 were missing. As you know this is the fifth time in a row that there has been a shortfall in the delivery. This causes us inconvenience, you extra expense and both of us aggravation. Could I suggest that you set up a meeting between us and your Warehouse Manager, to discuss what can be done to improve matters? If deliveries do not then improve, I regret we shall have to consider turning to a more reliable supplier.

In the meantime, please arrange for the balance to be supplied as soon as possible.

Yours sincerely

Helen Meeting
Office Manager

When mistakes are repeatedly being made, customers are justified in raising their hackles. The tone of the letter is one of irritation. But it doesn't seek to blame. Instead it points out the need to improve matters because everyone is suffering. Ranting and railing on its own is often pointless – it may feel good but it is usually better to suggest a constructive solution, or at least, as here, to sit down and talk about the issues.

The delays that have occurred here are not serious and the customer did not make it a condition of the contract that time should be of the essence. To start issuing threats of taking your business elsewhere, therefore, would not fit the circumstances. Nevertheless, the customer is being inconvenienced. A plea for the supplier to give it "your most urgent attention" should be sufficient to get the wheels moving.

Taylor Taylor & Shaw
Benton House, Clifton, Bristol BS16 7LJ
Tel: (0117) 1089254   Fax: (0117) 1089211

Mr N Stacey
N Stacey & Co Ltd
Amber House
Grant Mill
Bristol
BS6 4RE

16 September 1999

Dear Mr Stacey,

Our purchase order no. AB46972 dated 6 September
On the 6th September, we placed an order with your company for a portable air conditioner (model no A132487). Our purchase order no. is AB46972.

When the order was placed, I was informed that you were temporarily out of stock of this item but that you had more on order and we could expect delivery within one week.

When I contacted your office on the 13th September, I was told that the air conditioner would arrive the next day. Three days have now passed and there is still no sign of a delivery or an explanation from yourselves.

Please give this matter your most urgent attention.

Yours sincerely,

AW Taylor

Partners: AW Taylor & GS Taylor

Taylor Taylor & Shaw

Benton House, Clifton, Bristol BS16 7LJ
Tel: (0117) 1089254   Fax: (0117) 1089211

Mr N Stacey
N Stacey & Co Ltd
Amber House
Grant Mill
Bristol
BS6 4RE

28 September 1999

Dear Mr Stacey,

Re: Our order no. AB46972, dated 6 September

I wrote to you on the 16th September, chasing the above order for a portable air conditioner model no. A132487.

In spite of my letter and several phone calls, this order is still outstanding and is now very urgently required.

When placing the order on the 6th September, we were told there would be a delay of only four days. Four weeks have now passed without an explanation from yourselves. Please telephone me on receipt of this letter with a new and definite date for delivery.

You will understand that, as a business, we put a high premium on reliability. If I do not receive your call, or if further delays are expected, this order will be cancelled and our business will be taken elsewhere.

Yours sincerely

AW Taylor

Partners: AW Taylor & GS Taylor

The delay has now become unacceptable and it is fully justifiable to threaten to cancel the order.

When writing letters like this, it is a good ploy to make use of certain emotional triggers, such as "You will understand that, as a business, we put a high premium on reliability". This is designed to provoke the response 'but so do we'. If it has the right effect, the supplier will pull out all the stops to deliver the item on time or, at the very least, to tell the customer what the situation is immediately.

This letter is strongly worded but wisely stops short of using anger to make its impact felt.

Showing that you have already considered several times whether to complain, adds weight to your justification in complaining now. It tells the reader that you are not over-reacting but that your patience has been tested.

The overall message is clear: the salesman's behaviour is reflecting badly on his company, and has reached such a state that you want nothing whatever to do with it.

If the writer had been tempted to show his anger, it would have undermined his credibility and inclined the reader to take the matter less seriously.

IDENDEN INDUSTRIES
A division of Idenden Plc
Porter House, Hull HU7 4RF England

Tel 01482 119087 Fax 01482 119088
Registered in England No: 1218943

Mr L Hines
Managing Director
Banks & Banister Ltd
The Old Exchange
Cambridge Road
Brampton
Cumbria
CA4 7MK

17 April 1999

Dear Mr Hines

John Higgins
I had hoped that I would not have to write to you about the activities of your company representative John Higgins, but his behaviour finally leaves me no option.

He has persistently called our office in an attempt to sell us one of your photocopiers. He has been told repeatedly that we have no requirements for any photocopiers and that we are very happy with our existing supplier. Today, he called my secretary and claimed that he was a close friend so that he would be put through. I regard this behaviour as totally unprofessional. His only success to date has been to increase my resolve that we shall never buy anything from your company.

I trust that we shall not hear from Mr Higgins again, nor any other representative from your company.

Yours sincerely

David Rex
Director

PARKER
Glass Ltd

Unit 27 Willow Park
Christchurch, Dorset BH23 6MM
Tel: 01202 109111
Fax: 01202 109112

Reg. No: England 962578762
VAT No: 9120564

Mr P Hoat
Manager
Wayside Hotel
Riverside Walk
Christchurch
Dorset
BO4 2DD

24 July 1999

Dear Mr Hoat

Lunch at the Wayside Hotel on 23 July
Yesterday, I entertained three very important potential clients at your hotel, which, as your staff will confirm, I have visited on many occasions over the last two years.

It gives me no pleasure to say that the occasion was a shambolic disaster from start to finish.

1. It took a full fifteen minutes from placing our drinks order to being served with them - not a pleasant experience when all of us were parched.

2. We were not invited to take our seat in the dining room for a full 45 minutes after arriving.

3. The cold soup was spiced to a degree that was unbearable. No warning was given of this either in the menu or by the waiter.

4. One of the starters did not arrive until ten minutes after the others were served.

5. There was an unacceptable gap of 20 minutes between our finishing the starters and the main course arriving.

6. Two of the waiters, although not discourteous, did not show the attentiveness that is expected from a hotel of your class.

Had I realised that we would receive this kind of treatment I would not have entertained such important guests at your hotel. You have my assurance that I will not be entertaining or recommending anyone to eat there in future.

Yours sincerely

Frank Crasson

The disasters relayed in this letter reach the status of a catastrophe. Presenting the individual complaints as a list makes them appear far worse. Each one has been identified and will have to be accounted for. No amount of apology could undo the wrong. The strength of feeling is conveyed in the evocative phrase "shambolic disaster".

Hotels and restaurants live by their reputations and the manager will be well aware of the damage if his receives a bad name. He may not be too concerned if the writer doesn't eat there again but he will be concerned if lots of people are deterred from trying out the hotel.

Here is an abundance of effective phrases to use in situations where you want to be firm about an issue: "...not of merchantable quality..."; "...don't have a moral leg to stand upon..."; "...really should know better..."; "...It was not we who caused this problem..."; "It is time this matter was brought to a close"; "...in full and final settlement...". These are all strong phrases that add weight to the claim being made and will convince the other side that you mean business.

Thomas King & Palmer Ltd

serving the world

24 Fuller Road, Welling,
Kent DA16 7JP
Tel : (01322) 100132
Fax : (01322) 100178

Reg. No : England 1212298762
VAT No : 92905643

Mr S K Robinson
Sales Director
Wright & Robinson Ltd
43 Knights Drive
Kenilworth
Warwickshire
CV10 4ZN

13 June 1999

Dear Mr Robinson,

Our Purchase Order No. 346987; your Invoice No. 120786
Re your fax to our accounts manager of 10th April, regarding the dispute on this transaction, I shall deal with this matter. I am very sorry that you find yourself in the middle of this dispute.

As you know, quite simply, the list of names was not of merchantable quality as presented.

As you are also aware, the timings on mailings are always tight. Every mailer has to commit to print before the lists can be run. The stark alternative to reworking the list to make as much of it as possible mailable was to dump the mailing pieces prepared for the list. We would have needed a great deal more than a full credit to compensate for that. Re-working the list was the only option.

The list suppliers may not like our solution, but they do not have a moral leg to stand on. A list in this condition simply should not have been represented as a mailing list. As a regular mailer of international lists, we know what constitutes acceptable product, and this clearly did not. The list suppliers really should know better than to maintain that the original list rental should be paid in full. It was not we who caused this problem.

It is time this matter was brought to a close. We have always explained we are willing to pay the balance. Our final offer is therefore £112.55 + VAT in full and final settlement, made up as on the attached sheet. We will pay this on receipt of the credit note for £708.77 + VAT.

I look forward to hearing from you.

Yours sincerely

Arthur French
Marketing Director

CHAPTER TWO

Managing Customers

The Customer is King. But knowing that doesn't make it any easier when you have an awkward one to manage, or mistakes happen that need to be sorted. There can be few matters less pleasant than an irate customer, and few more gratifying than one who is satisfied. The letters in this chapter provide a wealth of ideas for keeping relations with customers on an even keel and, when the waters turn choppy, what you can do to calm them down again.

Saying sorry
It sounds simple, but how many customers genuinely believe what you say? Saying sorry sincerely, so that a customer decides to stay with you rather than move to your competition, is an art. Letter 29 is an example of one that genuinely worked.

Handling awkward customers
Difficult customers need to be handled carefully. Don't just ignore them even if they are rude, as in letter 30. And don't let them steamroller their way with you – be firm, as in letter 31.

The easiest source of new business?
Your existing customers are your easiest source of new business. They have used you once and, if they enjoyed the experience, they will come back to you again, and again. Taking the time and trouble to thank them may not seem a profitable use of your time but it will reap rewards. Letters 34–5 give some ideas.

Don't forget your lapsed customers
These ones are well worth trying to revive. You won't get them all back, but just a few will make the effort worthwhile. See letter 38.

'Ex-works' is a term that commonly occurs in quotations and means that the supplier makes the goods available from his premises. Unless stated otherwise, the purchaser is expected to arrange collection of the goods and organise any export licences and other documentation that may be required, as well as transportation. The purchaser assumes the full risk of damage to the goods, once the goods are in his control. For a precise understanding of the term ex-works (and other shipping terms), it is recommended that you consult a copy of the Incoterms which can be obtained from the International Chamber of Commerce, tel. 0171-823 2811.

Note again, the helpful advice that the supplier is giving: what additional costs will have to be borne; the fact it will be cheaper to transport the items by sea rather than air and when he is going to be unavailable.

⊛ WILSON SMITH LTD

A wholly-owned subsidiary of The Wilson Group PLC
16 Willow Walk, Retford, Nottingham NG6 8WS
Tel: (01777) 121211 Fax: (01777) 121233
Reg. No: England 1212298762

Mr Winston Pathmanathan
Director
Kuantan Industries
5 Ipoh Street
5100 Kuala Lumpur
Malaysia

20 July 1999

Dear Winston

I am pleased to quote you ex-works prices for the items, as requested. All are in excellent working order but, in some cases, I am offering you an alternative for new items. I cannot give you the total price until I know exactly what you require, as we will have to add inland haulage, packing and freight charges. Please let me know whether you want the items sent by sea or air freight. Given the bulk of some of them, sea would be cheaper.

1. Photocopiers @ £940.00 each.

2. IBM Typewriters - second-hand Golf Ball @ £90.00 each. New modern electronic @ £360.00 each.

3. Olympia manual typewriters - second-hand @ £105.00 each. New @ £300.00 each.

4. Fax machines - we can supply new or reconditioned second-hand @ £375.00 each. Obviously, the second-hand ones are sturdier machines with more functions than the new ones for the same price.

Please contact me as soon as possible, to let me know your requirements as I shall be away on annual leave for two weeks from 6th – 23rd August.

I look forward to hearing from you shortly.

Yours sincerely,

James Smith
Marketing Director

BELLS OF BASILDON

Bells of Basildon Ltd, Unit 12, Way Park, Basildon SS12 6DE
Tel: 01268 109 9954 Fax: 01268 109 5576 Reg. No. England 13078453 VAT No: 75698764

Mr J Bracket
Purchasing Manager
A S Charlwood Ltd
87 Main Street
Brentwood
Essex
CH7 8DC

16 June 1999

Dear Jim

What can I say? Sorry.

It seems a gremlin got into our wordprocessor and decided to move the decimal point over a little too far. The price should of course have been £2545 and not £254.50. We are doing our best to control the beast but it still occasionally steps out of line.

I hope, in spite of the apparent tenfold increase (!), that the price is still acceptable.

Yours sincerely

Terry Monk
Estimator

Here a situation has arisen, where a quoted price is significantly lower than it is in reality. The difference is so great that the customer may already realise it is a simple typographical error. Nevertheless, the supplier wants to retain the goodwill of the customer.

Making light of it in this way is not always appropriate: it all depends on how well you know your customer. Here, they get on very well, so the tone is fitting.

Passing the blame on to an imaginary 'gremlin' also cleverly diverts the attention away from the real cause of the mistake – yourself, perhaps.

The exclamation mark in brackets in the last sentence lightens what might otherwise be a rather solemn sentence.

Too many businesses take new customers for granted, even though they are like gold dust.

A letter of welcome should take the opportunity to give the customer the confidence that she has chosen the right company and is in safe hands.

Note how the business creates a good impression in the mind of the customer, by offering an additional service free of charge as a 'nice surprise'.

Expressions worth noting here are: "...a long and happy association..." and "...should we fall short of your high expectations...", which emphasise how much trouble your business is prepared to take to help and leaves the customer feeling comfortable with choosing you.

IDENDEN INDUSTRIES
A division of Idenden Plc
Porter House, Hull HU7 4RF England

Tel 01482 119087 Fax 01482 119088
Registered in England No: 1218943

Mrs J Holmes
Holmes and Barker Associates
23 Holly Bush Lane
Stretham
Cambs
CB8 4JK

16 August 1999

Dear Mrs Holmes

Interior fittings for 23 Holly Bush Lane
Many thanks for your order received today.

We are delighted that you have chosen us to supply you with interior fittings for your new premises. I hope that you will be pleased with the results of our work but, should you have any quibble, however small, please contact me and I will ensure that it is attended to immediately.

As part of our welcome pack for new clients, your order entitles you to have a free consultation, with a recommendation of how the workspace can be designed to the ergonomic advantage of your employees. This service is completely free to all customers placing their first order with us before the end of the year. If you would like to take advantage of this limited offer, please complete and return the enclosed card.

We look forward to a long and happy association with your business. Should we fall short of your high expectations in any matter, please contact me personally.

Yours sincerely

Stuart Jones
Sales Manager

⊛ WILSON SMITH LTD

A wholly-owned subsidiary of The Wilson Group PLC
16 Willow Walk, Retford, Nottingham NG6 8WS
Tel: (01777) 121211 Fax: (01777) 121233
Reg. No: England 1212298762

Mr Winston Pathmanathan
Director
Kuantan Industries
5 Ipoh Street
5100 Kuala Lumpur
Malaysia

30 November 1999

Dear Winston

Re Chambon machine
As requested, I enclose the specification and photograph of the Chambon machine, which we have on offer.

We currently have a potential buyer from Ghana, who is interested and has offered £50,000 ex-works. We are prepared to accept this offer and he will be looking at the machine next week, unless you are seriously interested and make a better offer. Please 'phone or fax me quickly, before I close the deal with this client.

I look forward to hearing from you.

Yours sincerely,

John Wilson
Sales Director

Just occasionally, you may find yourself in the happy position of having two customers competing for the same item, as here. It may not happen very often but it can do wonders for concentrating the customer's mind on the buying decision.

Here, the supplier signals that he is going to accept the highest bidder. A word of warning though, don't play this game unless you have someone else who is seriously interested — otherwise it could backfire on you badly. You should also bear in mind that the loser may feel ill will towards you. If you think a longer-term relationship may be jeopardised, it would be better to accept the first offer and tell the second client that the item is already sold.

This is a courteous, standard letter, notifying that an item on an order is out of stock. It doesn't have a personalised ring to it. The clue to this is that the title is not mentioned in the letter, only on the invoice. And no reference is made to the way the customer has actually paid – it says what happens depending on how he has paid.

A hint of personal attention comes through in the second paragraph, where a promise is made to be in contact if the order cannot be supplied within two weeks. Another nice touch is shown in giving a 'phone number to ring if there is a problem. This is on the letterhead anyway, but it makes the number easier to find and subtly reassures the customer.

Grange & Turner Ltd
32 WESTBOURN ROAD, WITNEY, OXON OX6 7HY

Telephone (01993) 107888
Fax (01993) 107843

Reg. No: England 13078453
VAT No: 75698764

15 St Patricks Road
Cottingham
Hull
HU5 3SR

12 August 1999

Dear Mr Black,

Your order 134987

Thank you for your recent order. I am afraid that we have temporarily sold out of the title indicated on the invoice.

New stocks have already been ordered and we expect delivery shortly. Of course, I will contact you again if I cannot despatch your book within the next two weeks.

If you have paid in advance, your cheque will not be banked until we have despatched all the items on your order. If you have paid by credit card, we will only debit for those items you have received so far.

All our books are supplied under our usual 10-day examination offer. If you have any further questions please do not hesitate to ring me on 01993 107888.

Please accept my apologies for this delay.

Your sincerely

Kevin Mason
General Manager

Grange & Turner Ltd

32 WESTBOURN ROAD, WITNEY, OXON OX6 7HY

Telephone (01993) 107888
Fax (01993) 107843

Reg. No: England 13078453
VAT No: 75698764

Mr H Mason
15 Longfield Road
Boars Hill
Oxford
OX568JH

24 February 1999

Dear Mr Mason,

Thank you for your letter dated 17th February addressed to our Managing Director, which has been brought to my attention. It is very nice to hear that you appreciate receiving our promotional material from time to time.

However, I am very sorry that you have been inundated with mailings to your son at your address. This has happened because he requested us to send goods to your address as above; with hindsight, we should have made sure that our computer was "flagged" no mailings on his name.

I would like to confirm that we have amended our records so that he will only receive his mailings at his Leighton Buzzard address and have arranged that only our literature is sent in future. You may receive unwanted mailings for about a month as there may be some in the pipeline but, after that period of time, they should stop.

Once again, please accept my apologies for the annoyance and inconvience caused. If you have any more queries please do not hesitate to contact me.

Yours sincerely

Jane Harvey
List Controller

The customer writing in obviously appreciates the service being offered and the tone of the letter fits the degree of the complaint. If there is a hint of good news in the complainant's letter it is well worth latching on to it, as here. It helps to remove some of the sting and put your company into a more positive light.

You still want to remedy the situation and, provided that you can take action or be seen to be taking action to satisfy the customer, you should not be troubled in the future.

When you are relying on a distributor or wholesaler for a product who in turn is relying on the main supplier overseas to supply an item, it is easy to find yourself the piggy in the middle between a customer and the people who can influence getting the product to you.

Obtaining reliable information about time-scales or delivery through the chain of suppliers is often difficult. When this occurs, your main line of defence with the customer has to be that you are applying pressure as regularly as possible.

H J KINGSLEY (NORWICH) LTD

Kingsley House, Morris Street, Norwich NR6 7JM
Tel: (01603) 117097 Fax: (01603) 117099 Reg. No: England 12086215 VAT No: 8793519

Mr F Goodge
Goodge, Turner and Weatherall
12 Macers Row
Holt
Norfolk
NR16 5TR

12 February 1999

Dear Mr Goodge

Axe accounting package

I am sorry that you have still not received this software package.

It is an American import which is distributed by a UK software house and there is a delay in getting stocks from the States. We are nagging the UK software house twice a week, who assure us that they are doing the same to their American colleagues.

I will keep you informed of progress.

Yours sincerely

Anne Goode (Mrs)
Sales Assistant

WILSON SMITH LTD

A wholly-owned subsidiary of The Wilson Group PLC
16 Willow Walk, Retford, Nottingham NG6 8WS
Tel: (01777) 121211 Fax: (01777) 121233
Reg. No: England 1212298762

Mr J West
General Manager
Idenden Industries
Porter House
Hull
HU7 4RF

16 May 1999

Dear Jim

Re: Delivery times

Thank you for returning the delivery cards: showing how long it is taking for our goods to arrive with you.

Your observation that deliveries seem to be taking longer than a year ago is correct. On average it is taking one extra day for goods to arrive with you, although our overall turnaround time from receiving your order to goods leaving the warehouse has not changed.

The cause of this extra time seems be the courier service we are currently using. We are, of course, concerned to offer you the best possible service, so for the next three months we shall be trying out an alternative service, to see if there is any improvement.

Please do continue to return the cards showing the date you receive the goods and please accept our sincere apologies for this slight deterioration in service.

Yours sincerely

Peter Grey
General Manager

Here, there is not a serious complaint, although the customer has noticed that goods are taking longer to arrive. The fault lies outside the direct control of the supplying company although it is within its power to amend, as it is the courier whose service has deteriorated.

The tone is conciliatory, without treating the situation as a big problem. "We are, of course, concerned...." is another useful phrase, helping to create the impression that you empathise with the reader and recognise the problem.

A customer may specify that a product must meet certain criteria. Unfortunately, he may not appreciate that meeting those criteria could have a knock-on effect elsewhere. Here the customer wants the inks to be tolerant of high temperatures *and* retain their glossy appearance. The key phrase here is "...I assure you this is perfectly normal and will not impede its function". "I trust everything is in order..." is a useful phrase to use when you are confident that what you are suggesting should satisfy the reader, but it still leaves the door open if they have any more queries.

WILSON SMITH LTD

A wholly-owned subsidiary of The Wilson Group PLC
16 Willow Walk, Retford, Nottingham NG6 8WS
Tel: (01777) 121211 Fax: (01777) 121233
Reg. No: England 1212298762

Mr Brian Adams
Production Director
FGH Products Ltd
Unit 8 Potters Lane Ind. Est.
Almondvale
Perth
PH1 2EL

29 September 1999

Dear Mr Adams,

Many thanks for the cheque for £394.00 received this morning, and I understand the reason for the delay in this payment.

I note that you were unhappy with the quality of some of the materials we sent and I would like to explain the situation. Your order specified that the product should be tolerant of high temperatures. The gloss version has a lower tolerance, which is why we supplied the matt to you. This is why the product may appear slightly rough although I assure you this is perfectly normal and will not impede its function.

I trust everything is in order and I look forward to being able to provide further quotations for you in the future.

Yours sincerely

Mike Rose
Sales Department

Grange & Turner Ltd

32 WESTBOURN ROAD, WITNEY, OXON OX6 7HY

Telephone (01993) 107888
Fax (01993) 107843

Reg. No: England 13078453
VAT No: 75698764

Mr W Holmes
154 High Road
Oakley
Oxford
OX7 8PL

21 June 1999

Dear Mr Holmes,

Re: The Power to Win

I was extremely concerned to hear that you have not received the above book, which should have been despatched to you a week ago.

I have made enquiries and have discovered that, in this instance, one of our internal procedural systems failed. This is a very rare occurrence (it happens about once a year although we continue to try to eradicate such mistakes entirely).

I can only ask that you accept our most sincere apologies for this inconvenience. To make amends, I am sending you a copy of the above book by special delivery. In addition, as you are a highly valued customer, I am enclosing a £5 voucher, which can be redeemed against any future order.

I do hope that this will go some way to restoring your faith in us.

Yours sincerely,

Susan Taylor
Customer Service Manager

When a customer complains, it is not just the current order that you may lose. That customer could be worth a lot of money to you over time – accounting for thousands of pounds of revenue during the time he does business with you.

If mistakes do happen your aim should be to mitigate the damage. Here, the supplier achieves this by reassuring the customer that it is a "...very rare occurrence...", supporting the claim with "...it happens about once a year...".

The customer is made to feel extra-special, with the remedy of having the item sent by special delivery, being referred to as a "...highly valued customer..." and being given a voucher for a discount off the next purchase – a cunning technique to tempt the customer back, which costs very little and boosts sales at the same time. Brilliant!

Some people's reaction to receiving an abusive letter is to bin the letter, because it obviously comes from a crank. But wait a minute. That person isn't reacting for no reason at all – he obviously feels very strongly about the issue. And, since he has cast aspersions on the reputation of your business, you should use the opportunity to set the record straight.

The first sentence tackles the abusiveness head-on. The phrase "In spite of your rude tone I will respond..." is designed to make him feel that you almost decided not to write and that he should appreciate that you have taken the trouble.

Note how the tone of the reply is cold and unapologetic. It offers a frank explanation without saying either "sorry" or "please accept our apologies".

PARKER
Glass Ltd
Unit 27 Willow Park
Christchurch, Dorset BH23 6MM
Tel: 01202 109111
Fax: 01202 109112

Reg. No: England 962578762
VAT No: 9120564

Mr S Wright
157 Colder Way
Basingstoke
Hants
BP6 5TG

12 December 1999

Dear Mr Wright,

It is not often I receive such an offensive letter. In spite of your rude tone I will respond to the issues you raised.

I understand that your letter is caused by your frustration at not being supplied immediately with the goods that you ordered. We take great pride in being able to supply all goods *held in stock* within 28 days at the latest. Our average turnaround time is, however, far shorter, at just nine working days. But there are occasions, such as this instance, when the demand for our goods is much greater than we anticipate. Normally we would simply reorder and aim to supply you within about two weeks. However, when the goods have to be imported from overseas, delays can be considerably longer. These are the circumstances that caused you such offence.

We are doing everything in our power to obtain the goods and supply them to you. I would like to reassure you that we shall not deduct the amount owed from your credit card until the day the goods are despatched to you. We always take complaints seriously and are ready to respond to all of them. I accept you feel strongly about this situation, but I would ask that any future correspondence between us is conducted in more appropriate language.

Yours sincerely

Peter Jones
Managing Director

IDENDEN INDUSTRIES
A division of Idenden Plc
Porter House, Hull HU7 4RF England

Tel 01482 119087 Fax 01482 119088
Registered in England No: 1218943

Jim Bone
Purchasing Manager
Wilson Smith Ltd
16 Willow Walk
Retford
Nottingham
NG6 8WS

12 February 1999

Dear Mr Bone

I am in receipt of your letter of 10 February.

You are claiming that if we do not deliver your goods ordered by 14 February that we shall be in breach of contract and you will cancel your order.

I would like to draw your attention to the agreement I set up with your predecessor, Malcolm Bute (see his letter dated 20 June 1997), which specifies that we shall only be in breach of contract if the goods are not supplied due to circumstances within our control. The industrial action at the distribution depot is clearly outside our control and we deny your claim to have the right to cancel the order.

We are doing everything in our power to compel our distributors to resolve the dispute swiftly. I am hopeful that the mediation being attempted will result in a speedy conclusion. I will ensure that your order is given priority, so that it is delivered to you at the earliest opportunity.

Yours sincerely

Michael Hardcastle
Sales Director

This is a tricky issue and one that would probably give the lawyers a field day. The legal issue is whether the prior contract set up with Mr Bone's predecessor overrides the contract which Mr Bone issued stating that "time was of the essence".

The legal issue aside, Michael Hardcastle clearly believes that he has a clear-cut case. The letter emphasises this belief, with phrases that are designed to knock his opponent off course: "I would like to draw your attention to the agreement..." and "...we deny your claim..." are examples. The only attempt to mollify Mr Bone occurs at the end, with the assurance that the order will be given priority.

This letter is firm but friendly in tone. The main paragraph takes a persuasive stance with the phrase "...the carriage charge is only a contribution towards the final cost of delivering the goods to you". It is worth noting how the request to pay gradually builds up, rising to a crescendo in the final sentence. Criticism of the charge itself is deflected by an acknowledgement that it is only a contribution towards the cost. Next comes the point that the customer's prevarication over the delivery address contributed to the adjustment having to be made. The customer is subtly made to feel indebted to the supplier because "...we do everything we can to keep the charges as competitive as possible...", which phrase is designed to counteract the pain that is inflicted with the information that the supplier can't "...absorb the cost...". Note how the formal request to pay comes right at the end of the letter, in a firm sentence with a diplomatic double negative: "...I do not consider it unreasonable...", a softer, less abrasive way of saying 'please pay'.

GKT Products Ltd, Unit 10, Castleway Lane, Alloway, Ayr, KA7 4BE
Telephone (01292) 177900 Fax (01292) 199855   Reg. No: 17964583 VAT No: 679845

Mr B Holmes
Marketing Manager
Beresford-Biggs Ltd
39 Cavalry Drive
Histon
Cambs
CB7 4FE

16 June 1999

Dear Bill,

Our estimate no 229674 and our invoice no. 113975
Thank you for your letter of 12 June, concerning the carriage charge on our invoice.

The document on which we gave you our price was clearly headed as an estimate, and not a quotation as you claim. This permits us to make any necessary adjustments. The adjustment of the carriage charge is only a contribution towards the final cost of delivering the goods to you. You may also recall that you were unable to provide us with details of where the goods were to be delivered, when you asked us to give you a price. While we do everything we can to keep the charges for our goods as competitive as possible, I regret that on this occasion we are unable to absorb the cost of delivery in our prices.

Given all these circumstances, I do not consider it unreasonable to ask you to pay the carriage charge and would appreciate it if you could settle the account by the end of this month.

Yours sincerely

Tony Bright
Customer Services Manager

RPP Holdings Plc
35/38 New Road, Paignton, Devon TQ3 4UU
Tel: 01803 175653 Fax: 01803 187908
Reg. No: England 1976143

Mr A D Nelson
Sales Manager
Healthaware Co Ltd
56 Barrow Street
St Albans
Herts
AL2 1LD

14 October 1999

Dear Mr Nelson,

Your order no. 29785
Thank you for your fax, which I received this morning, asking if it was possible to increase your print order from 10,000 to 15,000 copies.

Your brochure went to press yesterday. I am afraid it has not been possible, therefore, for us to print an additional 5,000 copies within the existing run and give you the benefit of a lower price. We can still print the extra copies, although they will be at the slightly higher reprint price we gave you. We could deliver these by next Wednesday. Do you still want us to go ahead?

The main run, I am pleased to say, is going smoothly and we are on course to deliver it to you on Friday.

Yours sincerely

George Stevens
Account Manager

Occasionally a customer will want to change his order while it is being processed. If this involves additional cost, you should stand by the original order. "I am afraid it has not been possible..." lets the customer down lightly. Your aim, though, should be to appear as helpful as possible. Note how the supplier explains that he can do the extra copies and gives a provisional delivery date.

If you decide to write an informal, jovial letter, make sure it doesn't overstep the mark. The person receiving this letter would need to be on very good terms with the sender.

In playing on the list of excuses that could have been made, there is a danger that the tone could be misconstrued and interpreted as being heavily sarcastic. The letter redeems itself, though, with the genuine note of thanks at the end.

Note how, even though the main paragraph has been written as a list, it is left as a piece of consecutive prose, which reflects how it would have been spoken. The numbers are there to emphasise, rather than separate, the text.

Fenner & Sons

16 George Street, Woodbridge,
Suffolk IP3 7KL
Tel: (01394) 198423
Fax: (01394) 198444
Registered in England: 91221299
VAT No: 919129075 80

Mr Bob Holmes
Senior Buyer
H J Kingsley (Norwich) Ltd
Kingsley House
Morris Street
Norwich
NR6 7JM

13 September 1999

Dear Bob

Just a note to say thank you for the cheque.

And how wonderfully refreshing, to receive a cheque the day after being told it is being sent!

Thank you for not: 1) passing the cheque on to a colleague on holiday for counter-signature, 2) despatching it to your Kings Lynn accounting centre for final approval and speedy processing, 3) including it in the next cheque run, 4) endeavouring to ensure it receives priority attention even though (a) Tuesday is too late in the week to be included in this week's cheque run, and (b) payments due after the 5th cannot normally be actioned in the same month.

In other words, hearty thanks.

Kind regards

John Smith
Accounts Manager

RPP Holdings Plc
35/38 New Road, Paignton, Devon TQ3 4UU
Tel: 01803 175653 Fax: 01803 187908
Reg. No: England 1976143

Mr David Cross
Sales Director
P P Plus Ltd
Grove Industrial Estate
Warwick
CV7 1PL

19 February 1999

Dear David

I am writing to thank you for recommending me to Peter Norman at DAS UK. Your kindness is very much appreciated.

If I remember rightly, you did, in fact, recommend me to this firm when they had offices in Kingston, although at the time nothing came of the enquiry.

We have put a price to them on a job of printing 4-colour process posters and, if anything comes of it, I will be in touch with you.

I hope that you are keeping well and busy; things are still very quiet here. We keep getting a lot of enquiries but many fall by the wayside when followed up. Anyway, we have survived two major recessions so we must be doing something right, and things are bound to pick up eventually.

I remember the last time I spoke to you that things were quiet at your end also; I hope things are now going better for you now.

Thank you once again for your kindness.

Yours sincerely

Richard Price
Director

If you end up getting business (or even the prospect of business) from a recommendation, it is not only courteous but also sound business sense to thank the person who recommended you. If you don't thank them, why should they bother to do it again? People like to feel appreciated and useful; it will make your associate more inclined to recommend you again in future. Ignoring the person who made the recommendation looks as if you are taking him for granted. Alternatively, he may think you didn't like the potential client and next time an opportunity comes along he will send it to a competitor!

If there is a gap between appointments, customers or suppliers may feel that their interests are not being looked after or they may notice a slip in service caused by the change-over. To prevent this happening it is worth announcing details of the new appointment and the date when the new person is due to join, in a personal letter. Emphasising how much experience they have gives confidence in the competence of the person. Offering a back-up or intermediate contact is also a good idea, in case an urgent matter arises before the appointee arrives.

Thomas King & Palmer Ltd
serving the world

24 Fuller Road, Welling,
Kent DA16 7JP
Tel : (01322) 100132
Fax : (01322) 100178

Reg. No : England 1212298762
VAT No : 92905643

Mr D Jenkins
Director
Chester Wood Ltd
35 Grand Hill Road
Waverton
Chester
CH6 5FG

30 August 1999

Dear Mr Jenkins,

New General Manager
We are pleased to announce the appointment of Gerald Best as General Manager from September 6th 1999. His appointment follows the retirement, due to ill health, of Tony March, in August.

Gerald comes to us with considerable experience of marketing and he will be contacting all of our clients as soon as he arrives, to introduce himself and to deal with any queries which may arise.

We are happy to assure all of our clients of the same, continuing, high-quality service for which we are proud to enjoy such a good reputation.

Should you, however, have any urgent enquiries, please do not hesitate to contact me personally.

Yours sincerely

Brian Moore
Director

Grange & Turner Ltd

32 WESTBOURN ROAD, WITNEY, OXON OX6 7HY

Telephone (01993) 107888
Fax (01993) 107843

Reg. No: England 13078453
VAT No: 75698764

Mr F V Bland
Director
Taylor, Taylor & Hall
25 Glebe Lane
Darlington
Co Durham
DL6 5TG

16 June 1999

Dear Mr Bland

As a company committed to providing a quality service, we like to keep in regular touch with your needs and your views of the products we produce and promote.

To maintain our high standard of quality products and service to you, I would be very grateful if you could complete the enclosed questionnaire.

In appreciation of your time, I shall be delighted to send you one of our superb quality Parker Pens on receipt of your completed questionnaire.

I look forward to receiving your reply and hope that we continue to be helpful to you in the future.

Yours sincerely

Mrs A Frank
Marketing Director

Gaining feedback from customers is essential. How else are you going to improve your service? Feedback from questionnaires can also provide some wonderful surprises – have you ever thought about using the favourable feedback as testimonials on future promotions? There is no more powerful seller of a product or service than a satisfied customer.

One difficulty with customer-attitude surveys is the comparatively low response they generate. A small, low-cost gift acts as an incentive and may increase the number of responses that you receive.

If you find customers buying once from you but not again, it can be worthwhile conducting a customer-service exercise to find out why they are not coming back to you. This letter dresses the investigation up to make it look like an after-sales service questionnaire. If you are asking for a large chunk of time, it may be worth sending a personalised letter in advance, explaining what you want to do and why.

Note how the letter empathises with the customer: "I appreciate this is a busy time for you..." and rather than asking her to 'phone you, announces that you will be in touch in a day or two. If you do say this, make sure not to leave it too long, so that the customer doesn't forget your letter.

H J KINGSLEY (NORWICH) LTD

Kingsley House, Morris Street, Norwich NR6 7JM
Tel: (01603) 117097 Fax: (01603) 117099 Reg. No: England 12086215 VAT No: 8793519

Ms Ruth Hope
Senior Buyer
Frank Fuller Ltd
34 Crester Street
Windrush
Oxon
OX7 9JU

2 October 1999

Dear Ruth,

I hope the last order we supplied to you was satisfactory and met your expectations.

We are currently looking at ways of improving our product range and services to our customers. I appreciate this is a busy time for you but I wonder if you would be prepared to spend half an hour discussing the service that you have received from us; what your expectations are about the products we supply; how those expectations have been met or exceeded and where you feel there is room for improvement. I would like to cover everything from initial supply of the order to the after-sales service that you have received.

I hope you are willing to help us in this matter. If I may, I will telephone you in a day or so to fix up a convenient date for us to meet.

Yours sincerely

Nina Davis
Marketing Manager

CHAPTER THREE

Debt Collection and Credit Control

Chasing for payment can be a soul-destroying activity, as customers either try to wriggle out of paying at all, or test your patience by seeing how long they can go without having to pay up. Many of the letters in this chapter are proven winners at getting recalcitrant customers to dig deep into their pockets and pay their dues. So you can be confident about using them, knowing that they have been genuinely tried and tested.

Choosing the right tone

Hitting the right note, first time, in a letter demanding payment, is not always easy. To help you choose, the collection letters have been divided broadly into three areas, as the Contents show: straightforward first-time demands for payment (letters 39 and 40); stronger demands (letters 41 and 42) and final demands that choose sterner phrases (letters 43 and 44).

Deterrents

If you want to try to avoid sending a letter chasing payment, the section on granting credit (letters 45–6) shows how to notify a new account of their terms of trading and offers a deterrent for you to try.

Handling a demand for payment

If you find yourself on the receiving end of a demand for payment, letter 50 shows how to keep the pack at bay for a little longer.

The tone of this collection letter is neutral. It is a simple enquiry, taking a non-confrontational standpoint.

Enquiring if there is a problem with the order is a subtle attempt to flush out any reasons for non-payment. Accounts departments are often the last to hear about any reasons why an invoice has not been paid. Note the fairly emphatic last sentence, not just asking when the invoice will be paid but for "...*immediate* settlement".

RPP Holdings Plc
35/38 New Road, Paignton, Devon TQ3 4UU
Tel: 01803 175653 Fax: 01803 187908
Reg. No: England 1976143

FAX MESSAGE TO: Janet Turner

FAX No: 015594 887766

FROM: Sue Frost - Accounts   DATE: 17 May 1999

OUR INVOICE NO. 115689 DATED 11.02.99
Our invoice no. 115689 dated 11.02.99, which refers to your order no. AL2158, should have been paid at the very latest by the end of April.

To date, we have not received your payment. I wonder if there has been a problem with this order of which we are not aware?

If not, please arrange immediate settlement.

Many thanks

Sue Frost

THIS MESSAGE CONSISTS OF ONE PAGE. PLEASE LET ME KNOW BY PHONE OR FAX IMMEDIATELY IF ANY PAGE IS ILLEGIBLE.

Tyler & Piper Associates

76 Whites Lane, Stevenage, Herts SG1 8JP England
Tel: (01438) 186465 Fax: (01438) 164323

Mr P Street
International Sales Manager
Hughes & Hickle Ltd
5 Bedford Way
Milton Keynes
MK55 6JJ

23 September 1999

Dear Mr Street

Commission Invoice No: 119747

I would like to remind you of our Export Consultation Agreement and draw your attention to the clients below who placed orders in 1998. A 10% commission is now outstanding.

Holz Engineering (Germany)	£32,047.05
Pierres (France)	£21,106.17
Jolon Export/Import Co. (Burma)	£43,844.00
TOTAL	£96,997.22
Total Commission due @ 10%	£ 9,699.72

We are, therefore, looking forward to the receipt of your cheque for the above sum by return.

Yours sincerely,

John Dunn
Financial Manager

Partners: DA Tyler BA & SR Piper MA

New arrangements that require a special payment – for example, a commission as in this case – can be easy to forget, particularly if it is due only once a year. A reminder is almost certainly necessary.

Where the amount owing is a percentage of a larger sum, don't forget to list each contract, calculate the total, and show how the percentage was arrived at. If the company here had simply issued an invoice for £9,699.72, there would have been no way of telling how that sum had accrued.

This letter strikes a polite tone, although it contains a veiled threat. The seriousness is conveyed by stating that the letter has been sent by recorded delivery (to nullify any excuse that it was not received and must have been 'lost in the post').

Signing the letter 'Legal Department' (even though the signatory may not be a lawyer) is designed to apply further pressure.

It is clear that legal action will be taken, but note how this is not made explicit, only implied in the euphemism "...passed into other hands...". Another effective phrase that can be applied in similar letters is "...render this action unnecessary...".

Charles Cunningham Ltd

29 Baker Street, LONDON N34 6GH England
Tel: (0171) 015 1290 Fax: (0171) 015 1271
Reg. No: England 1104398135 VAT No: 82108643

By Recorded Delivery

Hugh Buggs
Financial Director
Edwards & Davis Ltd
Western HouseBridge Street
Preston
Lancs
PR5 3FD

19 May 1999

Dear Mr Buggs,

I am surprised to have received no reply to our previous letter, asking for immediate settlement of the attached statement, which is long overdue.

Unfortunately, I cannot allow this account to remain unpaid any longer, and I regret that the matter will be passed into other hands in seven days.

I am still hopeful that you will render this action unnecessary by sending your remittance in full to arrive here within seven days.

Yours sincerely,

Keith Vail
Legal Department

**Wright &
Simpson**

157 Colder Way
Basingstoke
Hants RG21 5TG
Tel: (01256) 125907
Fax: (01256) 190986

Eric Barker
Director
Charles Cunningham Ltd
29 Baker Street
London
N34 6GH

9 March 1999

Dear Mr Barker

Thank you for your fax, regarding payment for your orders.

Our bank details are:

National Westminster Bank
Acc No: 46789124   Sort Code: 00 12 34

I must say that I regard your statement that we should "expect payment in
approximately two weeks" as extremely disappointing.

Outstanding Amount: £768.54   Invoice Nos: 316789 & 316790

The above invoices are dated 23 January and on our 30-day terms were due for
payment by 28 February. As these payments are already overdue, I do not see why
we should tolerate a further two weeks' delay; we have still to hear when one of the
invoices might be paid at all.

I would like, at the very least, a firm commitment for the latest date we can expect
payment – preferably well within the two weeks.

I look forward to hearing from you.

Yours sincerely

Mary Taylor
Customer Account Manager

P.S. We supplied our bank details as you requested in January "in order that
payment for the above invoices could be made as soon as possible".

Partners: EG Wright MA & FA Simpson

Quoting the words of the debtor back at him is a valuable technique for inducing payment. The person is made to feel that he is not to be trusted, having broken his promises.

Note some of the emphatic phrases that intensify the meaning behind a sentence: "I must say..."; "...I do not see why..."; "...have still to hear..."; I would like at the very least...". All these strengthen the thrust of the letter.

'We've been rumbled' would be the response of the recipient of this letter (if the business was in genuine trouble). If the suspicion of insolvency is unfounded on the other hand, it should provoke a firm rebuttal – no genuine business likes to get this kind of reputation because it is going to dent its credit rating severely.

An interesting point worth noting is the use of a specific time and day for payment to be received. If the writer had put "...received payment by Tuesday 21 November...", the creditor would not be able to take action until first thing Wednesday. Putting a specific time limit means that appropriate action can be taken at one minute past noon on the Tuesday. A small point, but one worth remembering if you are very anxious to get your money back. Setting a time limit also makes you sound more determined – as if your lawyers are lined up, ready and waiting to be sent in.

Charles Cunningham Ltd

29 Baker Street, LONDON N34 6GH England
Tel: (0171) 015 1290 Fax: (0171) 015 1271
Reg. No: England 1104398135 VAT No: 82108643

Mr E Wright
Senior Partner
Wright & Simpson
157 Colder Way
Basingstoke
Hants
RG6 5TG

12 November 1999

Dear Mr Wright,

Our Undisputed Invoice No. 005694
Your account has been passed to me for attention, because we are receiving from your business the classic signals of one about to go under. Apparently, our phone messages are not responded to, and the only member of your staff we can speak to is a temp, who is unable to provide any answers.

I sincerely hope that this is not the case, and that there is some misunderstanding which can be easily explained.

But we are owed £3652.00 for our undisputed invoice no. 005694, relating to your order no. BNN5643. And payment was due at the end of September.

To avoid any further misunderstanding, please forward your payment by return.

Please treat this as a formal and final request. If we have not received payment by noon on Tuesday 21 November, legal proceedings will commence without further notice to you.

Yours sincerely,

Keith Vail
Legal Department

RPP Holdings Plc
35/38 New Road, Paignton, Devon TQ3 4UU
Tel: 01803 175653 Fax: 01803 187908
Reg. No: England 1976143

Mrs Jane Markham
Finance Director
Grange & Turner Ltd
32 Westbourn Road
Witney
Oxon
OX6 7HY

27 February 1999

Dear Mrs Markham

Re. Outstanding account
Thank you for your cheque for £1500 in partial settlement of your account.

We appreciate this act of good faith but, regrettably, this amount does not clear your account and leaves £1297.98 still outstanding on invoices that are now 76 days overdue for payment.

We shall give you seven days from the date of this letter to settle your account. If we have not received payment in full by that date, we shall instigate court proceedings to recover the sum.

Yours sincerely

Tom Richards
Finance Director

Some customers may try to buy time to pay off their debts. They may have genuine difficulties that can be solved in time and a more conciliatory approach may be appropriate.

But if they have not provided you with a satisfactory reason for the delay and you suspect that they are simply playing for time, this type of letter may be necessary. It contains some good phrases: "We appreciate this act of good faith…" and "…regrettably, this amount does not clear your account…".

When a new account is opened, the terms of trading should have been agreed in advance.

Before accepting an order on a credit basis, the company should take up trade references and conduct a credit check, to ensure there is a good prospect of receiving payment. The company should then confirm that a credit account has been opened, as in the letter here.

This is a good opportunity to inform the customer about individual operating procedures, which will lead to a harmonious business relationship and reduce the chance of nasty surprises being sprung.

B & R HENDERSONS LTD
Marlows Road, Aberdeen AB20 5GT
Tel: 01224 267855 Fax: 01224 267977
Reg. No: 16497811 VAT No: 7387945

Helen Mitchell
Sales Manager
Good & Peabody
34 Kiln Street
Aberdeen
Scotland
AB8 7HY

13 August 1999

Dear Ms Mitchell

Thank you for returning our credit application form.

I have pleasure in informing you that a credit-trading account has been opened for you, with a limit of £3000 as requested. For your information, here are a few important points concerning our operating procedures:

1. Office hours are 8.30am to 5.30pm inclusive, Monday to Friday.

2. Orders are dispatched by carrier on a three-working-day service. This means that for orders received by, for example, 12 noon on Monday, delivery will be on Thursday.

   2.1 Next-day delivery is available, at an extra cost.

3. A detailed, but un-priced, delivery note is included in each consignment.

4. Invoices are posted at the time of dispatch and often arrive ahead of the goods.

5. Your sales contact is either Sue Spreadborough or Richard Selby but, for your convenience, all of our staff can accept telephone orders.

6. The threshold for carriage-paid orders is £500, although we have no minimum order quantity. A carriage charge will be levied for small orders.

Please do no hesitate to contact me, should you require further information.

Yours sincerely

Peter Lee
General Manager

IDENDEN INDUSTRIES
A division of Idenden Plc
Porter House, Hull HU7 4RF England

Tel 01482 119087 Fax 01482 119088
Registered in England No: 1218943

Mr B Holmes
Marketing Manager
Beresford-Biggs Ltd
39 Cavalry Drive
Histon
Cambs
CB7 4FE

16 July 1999

Dear Mr Holmes

Credit surcharge
As I am sure you are aware, the current economic climate is pressurising supplier and customer alike. The continued high cost of credit now means that we are obliged to insist upon prompt payment of our sales invoices, within the agreed terms of 30 days net.

A 5% credit surcharge will apply to all sales invoices from 3rd August.

A value of an equal amount will be allowed as a prompt payment discount, provided that full payment is received within 30 days of date of invoice.

This will be rigorously applied, as we can no longer fund the extended credit that a small percentage of our customers is abusing.

You have placed an order for wing nuts with us; before we process this further, I am obliged to seek your written agreement to our terms of trading.

Please sign this amendment to our terms of trading and return it without delay.

Yours sincerely

John Goodge
Finance Director

I agree to the application of a credit surcharge of 5% on all my invoices and I agree that, in the event of my payment exceeding the 30 days limit, I shall not deduct the surcharge but accept it as a valid invoice item and remit the debt in full.

Signed B Holmes.............................

For Beresford-Biggs Ltd   Date:

This type of letter is likely to raise a few hackles and may prove controversial with some of your better-established customers. Attempting to change general terms and conditions once trading has begun is bound to produce some resistance. When the terms affect the amount that (potentially) has to be paid, it is likely to produce some waves. You must be prepared to lose some customers who prefer to obtain their supplies elsewhere.

The advantage of this term is that those who do pay on time should not really have any reason to object, since it is not directed at them, while if they are likely to be affected you should be questioning whether to do business with them anyway.

Note the need to obtain the written agreement of your customers to introduce the term.

Occasionally, a customer may get into cash-flow difficulties and notch up a record of poor payment. Even though the cash-flow problems may be temporary, it is prudent to consider withdrawing the credit terms that the customer was previously permitted.

Note in this letter how the supplier makes it explicit when the goods will be despatched, not simply when the cheque has been received but when it has cleared through the account.

The final sentence should help to take some of the sting out of the mistrust that is conveyed – although the customer has only himself to blame.

⊗ WILSON SMITH LTD

A wholly-owned subsidiary of The Wilson Group PLC
16 Willow Walk, Retford, Nottingham NG6 8WS
Tel: (01777) 121211 Fax: (01777) 121233
Reg. No: England 1212298762

Mr Brian Adams
Production Director
FGH Products Ltd
Unit 8 Potters Lane Ind. Est.
Almondvale
Perth
PH1 2EL

29 September 1999

Dear Mr Adams,

Re your order no. TE3156
Thank you for the above order.

Your previous payment record precludes us from offering you our normal credit terms. We therefore enclose our pro forma invoice No. BN8164 for £456.76.

If you would like to send us a bank draft for the amount or arrange a credit transfer to our account, we shall gladly supply you with the items ordered by return.

Alternatively, we can accept a cheque, although the goods will not be despatched until the amount has cleared through our account.

We regret having to impose these stringent terms on you and hope that we may soon be able to resume a normal trading relationship.

Yours sincerely

Jim Tay
Finance Director

RPP Holdings Plc
35/38 New Road, Paignton, Devon TQ3 4UU
Tel: 01803 175653 Fax: 01803 187908
Reg. No: England 1976143

Attn. Brian O'Neil
Taylor & Shaw Ltd
Grafton Way
Exeter
Devon
EX447MB

27 January 1999

Dear Sir

We note that you have failed to respond to our previous demands to settle the debt of £34.80 that you owe this company

Should you ever wish to receive items from this company in the future, it will give us great pleasure to refuse you.

Yours faithfully

Tom Richards
Finance Director

This is a variation of a letter asking a customer not to come back, ever.

The phrase "...it will give us great pleasure..." sounds as if it is preceding a compliment so it is a shock for the reader when the compliment turns into a pointed insult. Its meaning is clear and uncompromising and no one receiving such a letter will be in any doubt about the intention.

If you are asked for details about an invoice, try to give as much information as possible: not only the invoice number, but also the customer's purchase order number, its date and, if possible, the name of the person who placed the order.

Thomas King & Palmer Ltd

serving the world

24 Fuller Road, Welling,
Kent DA16 7JP
Tel : (01322) 100132
Fax : (01322) 100178

Reg. No : England 1212298762
VAT No : 92905643

Frank O'Neil
Marketing Manager
Benton Copleys
Roundtree House
Kennet
Newmarket
CB8 7LP

25 June 1999

Dear Frank,

Thank you for your fax dated 20 June.

I enclose a copy of our Invoice No. 85930 as requested. These items were ordered against your Purchase Order No. 45844, dated 1 May and signed by Hazel Partridge.

I hope this clears up the matter but, if you do have any other queries, please do not hesitate to contact me.

Yours sincerely

Bill Vail
Accounts Manager

RPP Holdings Plc
35/38 New Road, Paignton, Devon TQ3 4UU
Tel: 01803 175653 Fax: 01803 187908
Reg. No: England 1976143

FAX MESSAGE TO: Mr M Wong, Financial Director

FAX No: (852) 2189 3698

FROM: T. Richards, Financial Director DATE: 4 October 1999

THIS MESSAGE CONSISTS OF ONE PAGE. PLEASE LET ME KNOW BY PHONE OR FAX IMMEDIATELY IF ANY PAGE IS ILLEGIBLE.

RE: YOUR INVOICE No 118597 DATED 7 AUGUST 1999

MESSAGE: I have today sent by international courier a cheque in the amount of £1070, in full settlement of the above invoice.

I am extremely embarrassed over the long delay – a result, I am afraid, of our accounting department not being as familiar as I am (and as they should be) with currencies other than the US Dollar.

Please accept my assurances that we will do everything to ensure that this kind of delay is not repeated in future. I hope we haven't done our reputation too much harm.

Regards

Tom Richards
Finance Director

This is a pleasant, disarming letter. It sounds completely genuine. Saying you are "...extremely embarrassed..." should put the other side off their guard. Blaming your accounts department is OK (provided you won't get into their bad books). "I hope we haven't done our reputation too much harm" demonstrates your concern and how much you empathise with your supplier's plight.

If you think you may need to use the services of your lawyer, it is best to ask in advance what sort of bill you are likely to incur in recovering the debt. This will probably influence your decision about whether to take legal action or how far down the road to go.

The lawyers may be a bit cagey on costs, because a lot will depend on the time needed. If they sound unwilling to give you a indication, ask what their hourly charging rate is. Having an idea in advance, and warning a lawyer of impending action, will save you time if you need to instruct them quickly.

H J KINGSLEY (NORWICH) LTD

Kingsley House, Morris Street, Norwich NR6 7JM
Tel: (01603) 117097 Fax: (01603) 117099 Reg. No: England 12086215 VAT No: 8793519

Mr J H Jones
Jones, Turner & Hills Partners
34 Frost Avenue
Norwich
NR3 7TF

23 June 1999

Dear Mr Jones,

Re: JW Mann (Packagers) Ltd
We have an outstanding debt of £12,501.90 with JW Mann (Packagers) Ltd. We have sent them a final demand for payment but I have heard on the grapevine that they are experiencing some severe cash-flow difficulties and I am not hopeful that we shall receive payment within seven days.

If we do not receive payment in that time, I would like to instruct your firm to issue proceedings against JW Mann. Before we do, though, I would appreciate an estimate of the foreseeable costs (including your disbursements) that we are likely to incur, assuming our claim is undisputed.

If you are unable to give us an estimate, please give us details of the hourly charging rate of your firm and, from your experience, a rough approximation of the number of hours that a case of this nature might take.

I am confident that our case is very strong and that no credible defence will be made to our claim.

Yours sincerely

Tim Good
Finance Director

CHAPTER FOUR

Employing People

A scan of the letters contained in this chapter shows the diversity of employee-related subjects that demand correspondence. Some of them are fairly straightforward, such as asking a candidate to attend an interview. Others, such as contracts, dismissals and maternity letters, require more consideration to make sure the correct legal regulations are being adhered to satisfactorily. All of them need to be carefully drafted if they are not to be misinterpreted by the recipient. Some of the highlights are examined here.

References

Giving references can be awkward, because of the need to give a fair and honest reply which does not conceal relevant information. A failure to do this could expose you to a claim from either the prospective employer or the employee. Letter 56 shows how to give a qualified reference.

Dismissal

Great care needs to be taken before dismissing someone without giving them a warning. Letter 58 shows how to handle it for a case of gross misconduct. Remember, this letter may be used in evidence against you in an industrial tribunal.

Condolences

For many people, a letter of condolence is one of the most difficult ones to write. But, at some time or other, most managers will have to face writing one. Letters 68–9 show how it can be done.

This approach strikes a fairly formal tone. Note how it sets a time and date for a candidate and asks her to confirm whether this is convenient. If you want to influence the schedule of interviews, use this letter. Most candidates will be inclined to agree to the time that suits you.

Fenner & Sons

16 George Street, Woodbridge,
Suffolk IP3 7KL
Tel: (01394) 198423
Fax: (01394) 198444
Registered in England: 91221299
VAT No: 919129075 80

Mrs F Godfrey
Woodland Green
Framlingham
Woodbridge
Suffolk
IP13 9PL

23 June 1999

Dear Mrs Godfrey,

Thank you for your application of 24 June for the post of Office Manager.

I would like to discuss the position in more detail with you and would be grateful if you could attend an interview at this office on Thursday 30 June at 10am.

Please confirm whether this time is convenient for you.

Yours sincerely

Brian Goodge
Personnel Manager

Grange & Turner Ltd

32 WESTBOURN ROAD, WITNEY, OXON OX6 7HY

Telephone (01993) 107888
Fax (01993) 107843

Reg. No: England 13078453
VAT No: 75698764

Mr S K Robinson
43 Knights Drive
Kenilworth
Warwickshire
CV10 4ZN

13 June 1999

Dear Mr Robinson,

Thank you for your letter of 3 June, enquiring if we have any vacancies for a personal assistant.

Unfortunately, all our situations are filled at present. However, we shall keep your letter on file and, should circumstances change, we shall contact you.

Yours sincerely

Yvonne Mitchelle
Personnel Department

Letters sending in speculative applications deserve, at the very least, this kind of reply. It doesn't need to be long but it puts the recipient clearly in the picture – even if the phrase "...we shall keep your letter on file..." followed by the promise to renew contact if circumstances change, is a promise that is rarely kept. Nevertheless, it shows willing but also demonstrates to the reader that he must look elsewhere for employment. Not bothering to respond to a speculative application shows a complete lack of courtesy and regard for the applicant.

If you have a very good candidate who you have to turn down, it may not be appropriate to write the applicant one of your standard letters of rejection.

This letter is a much friendlier way of turning the applicant down and shows at the same time that you know she came very close to the mark. Note how the letter makes it clear to the candidate that she has not been successful, to avoid any ambiguity.

If the person was particularly outstanding she may be someone that you want to consider for the future, so offering to keep her name on file gives her some hope that the application was not in vain and, at the same time, lets her down more lightly.

H J KINGSLEY (NORWICH) LTD
Kingsley House, Morris Street, Norwich NR6 7JM
Tel: (01603) 117097 Fax: (01603) 117099 Reg. No: England 12086215 VAT No: 8793519

Mrs E Robinson
Downhill Cottage
Hingham
Norwich
Norfolk
NR9 4FG

23 January 1999

Dear Mrs Robinson,

Thank you for attending the interview last week for the post of Office Manager.

The standard of applicants has been very high and, after careful consideration, I regret that you have not been successful on this occasion. It is unfortunate that we could not appoint two people to this position, as your experience matches the requirements very closely. In view of this, I would like to keep your name on file and, should a similar position occur in the future, would be pleased to consider you again, should you also be interested.

In the meantime, thank you for the interest you have shown in our company and I would like to wish you personally every success in your future.

Yours sincerely

P J Cross
Personnel Manager

H J KINGSLEY (NORWICH) LTD

Kingsley House, Morris Street, Norwich NR6 7JM

Tel: (01603) 117097 Fax: (01603) 117099 Reg. No: England 12086215 VAT No: 8793519

Mr John Price
45 Beeches Road
Thorpe St Andrew
Norwich
NR7 0LK

9 February 1999

Dear John,

Following our conversation this morning, I am delighted to confirm our offer of the job of Office Manager, with effect from Monday 29 February 1999.

I confirm that your annual salary will be £16,000, which will be paid monthly in arrears. Your salary will be reviewed after six months, in August. Thereafter, it will normally be reviewed annually in April.

The post reports to John Hibbert, our Managing Director. Our normal terms of employment will apply, as outlined on the attached sheet. We do operate a sick-pay scheme and, although we do not have a company pension scheme, we give every help to anyone wishing to set up a personal scheme.

Your normal hours each week will be 9.00am to 5pm, Monday to Friday, with an hour's break for lunch.

You will be entitled to 20 days holiday per year in addition to statutory holidays and the three days between Christmas and New Year. One month's notice is required on either side, and the first three months are viewed as a mutual trial period.

Your employer, for contractual purposes, is H J Kingsley (Norwich) Ltd.

Please sign the attached copy in acceptance of this offer.

Yours sincerely

P J Cross
Personnel Manager

I accept the above offer of employment as set out in the above letter.

Signed .... Date ....

Offers of employment may vary from those that are highly detailed contracts, to those that contain the minimum of legally required information. A letter that contains all the details of a contract could appear intimidating to some employees and may even deter some candidates at the last minute. This letter allows the writer to adopt a friendlier but no-less-professional approach.

The points that need to be stated in a contract are: the position, the date of joining, the name of your employer, the salary, how frequently the salary is paid, when it will be reviewed, the normal hours of work, amount of holiday, rights to sick pay, pension arrangements, the period of notice that is required on either side and to whom the post reports.

You will want the employee to confirm their appointment in writing with you. Note how a duplicate copy is enclosed for the employee to sign and return, saving him the trouble of having to sit down and compose a letter.

If there has been an incident (a disciplinary offence, for example) that is asked about you should not ignore it in a reference. Note how the letter seeks to put the offence into its true context - it was a one-off and his performance apart from that one time has been exemplary.

Don't be afraid to state exactly how you interpret a particular question. Here the former employer is unaware of all the responsibilities expected of the candidate in his new job, so note how the question is thrown back with the phrase "...provided appropriate training is made available to him..." which cleverly leaves the new employer with the responsibility for making the judgement.

Thomas King & Palmer Ltd

serving the world

24 Fuller Road, Welling,
Kent DA16 7JP
Tel : (01322) 100132
Fax : (01322) 100178

Reg. No : England 1212298762
VAT No : 92905643

Sarah Milnes
Personnel Manager
Charles Cunningham Ltd
29 Baker Street
London
N34 6GH

8 March 1999

Dear Ms Milnes,

Thank you for your letter requesting a reference for John Hibbert.

I can confirm that John held the position of Office Assistant with us for just over three years, from June 1996 to Jan 1999.

John's time-keeping was excellent and, although he had the occasional day off sick in a year, the amount was no more than one would expect. Most of the occasions were caused by seasonal bouts of 'flu.

Although John is a conscientious worker, he was disciplined on one occasion for taking an additional day's holiday over and above his normal entitlement. This incident was very much an exception and I have never had cause to complain about any other matter.

I am not aware of all the responsibilities that you are expecting him to perform but, provided appropriate training is made available to him, I would say that John is now ready to build upon his current experience and take on more responsibility in his new appointment.

He has a very affable personality and the ability to work well in a team environment, especially where it is essential to get on with a number of different types of people. I have every confidence he will make a valuable contribution to your business and am therefore pleased to be able to support his application.

Yours sincerely

Peter Holmes
Personnel Manager

GKT Products Ltd, Unit 10, Castleway Lane, Alloway, Ayr, KA7 4BE
Telephone (01292) 177900 Fax (01292) 199855   Reg. No: 17964583 VAT No: 679845

Mr Richard Green
Barton Close
Alloway
Ayr
KA7 4GB

16 April 1999

Dear Mr Green,

Many thanks for your telephone call concerning your disability. I am very sorry to hear about this and trust that something can be done to alleviate the pain and discomfort.

In the circumstances it would appear that you can no longer carry out your contract work for us as an Engineer and Consultant. I therefore regret that we must terminate our agreement, with immediate effect.

Perhaps you could keep in touch with me? If your health situation improves, let me know and we shall be pleased to review your contract.

Yours sincerely,

Mark Winters
Contracts Manager

The person here is not an employee as such but was working on a freelance basis for the company. The letter adopts a suitably concerned tone for the business relationship.

Although the recipient knows that he can no longer perform his contractual duties, the writer is keen to soften the impact of the termination of the agreement, by ending on an optimistic note which willingly offers the prospect of renewing the contract. Note how the writer doesn't commit himself as such – but instead offers to "review" the contract.

A summary dismissal can be difficult to defend at an industrial tribunal and a decision to dismiss instantly should not be taken lightly. If you do decide to dismiss, you must demonstrate that you have given the employee every opportunity to explain his conduct. A failure to do this may lead to a claim for unfair dismissal.

Note how a description of the sequence of events is built into the letter, showing that the dismissal was not instantaneous but occurred 24 hours after the event.

Grange & Turner Ltd
32 WESTBOURN ROAD, WITNEY, OXON OX6 7HY

Telephone (01993) 107888
Fax (01993) 107843

Reg. No: England 13078453
VAT No: 75698764

Mr John Black
34 Green St
Cheltenham
Gloucestershire
GL51 7HY

13 June 1999

Dear Mr Black,

On 12 June at 1.30pm, you were discovered in the Managing Director's office, using an unauthorised password to access the personnel files on the Managing Director's personal computer. You knew that this information was confidential and sensitive and that you were not permitted access to this data.

You were sent home immediately on a 24-hour suspension and invited the next day to come back to give an explanation of your conduct. At that meeting, on 13 June, you claimed that you were borrowing the computer to type a letter as your own computer was temporarily not functioning. No evidence of the letter that you alleged you were typing on the machine was produced. Your own computer was checked and found not to have any fault. There were also at least three other computers near your office that you could have chosen to use. In addition, the Managing Director's computer records the precise time and date when the password to the personnel files has been used. It shows that access to these files was obtained between 1.19pm and 1.33pm. This password was intended to be known only to the Managing Director and his personal assistant. Neither of them were in the building that day.

You have betrayed the trust, confidence and responsibility that the Company expects of a departmental manager. Your actions were well outside the bounds of what you were employed to do and amount to gross misconduct. For this reason, we have no option but to dismiss you, with immediate effect.

Yours sincerely

John Tome
Personnel Director

Charles Cunningham Ltd

29 Baker Street, LONDON N34 6GH England
Tel: (0171) 015 1290 Fax: (0171) 015 1271
Reg. No: England 1104398135 VAT No: 82108643

Mr Michael Tooke
UK Sales Manager

31 March 1999

Dear Michael,

Profit-sharing scheme, Financial Year 1998/9

I am delighted to report that we have had an excellent year and I would like to take this opportunity to thank you personally for all the hard work that you have put in over the last 12 months. The launch of the new range of products has helped to contribute to the growth of the company, and we anticipate this growth increasing during the forthcoming year as newer products become available.

Our turnover is up 10 per cent at £2,960,613 and profit before tax is up 12 per cent on last year at £298,415. Under the terms of our profit-sharing scheme, 5 per cent of the profits are eligible to be distributed amongst all the staff in proportion to each person's salary. I am therefore pleased to announce that £497 has been added to your salary this month.

Thank you once again for your contribution to the company this year. We have already got off to a tremendous start and I hope to be able to announce an even larger profit figure for next year, which, of course, will translate into a larger profit-share payment for you.

Good luck.

Yours sincerely

Derek Law
Managing Director

With good news for employees, you want to try and capitalise on it as much as possible and show how much you appreciate everyone's efforts in achieving these results.

The phrases "...thank you personally for all your hard work..." and "Thank you once again for your contribution..." help get that message across in a more individual-sounding and less corporate way.

Note how the letter looks forward to the future, laying out a vision of a better bonus in the following year, which helps to motivate the staff and give them something to work towards.

Conscientious employees who are off sick for long periods will be concerned about what the company thinks about their time off. This type of letter needs to blend the personal message of sympathy with the 'corporate line'.

The expressions of concern for the employee's health are sandwiched between the corporate policy on sick pay, but they help to bring the correspondence on to a more personal and sympathetic footing. Phrases such as "I do hope you make a swift recovery..." and "...wish you well" are good ones to remember when writing these letters.

RPP Holdings Plc
35/38 New Road, Paignton, Devon TQ3 4UU
Tel: 01803 175653 Fax: 01803 187908
Reg. No: England 1976143

Mrs Sarah Thompson
27 Beacon Close
Paignton
Devon
TQ3 6UJ

14 June 1999

Dear Sarah,

I am very sorry to hear that you are still not making a good enough recovery to be able to return to work.

I have heard in the meantime from your doctor, who says that she does not think you will be fit enough to return to work for at least six months, although she would, obviously, like to keep the situation under review.

You asked me how this news affects your entitlement to pay. Under our employment contract, you are entitled to four weeks' genuine illness within a year at full pay. You are then entitled to a further four weeks at three-quarters of your pay, and a further 18 weeks at a quarter of your pay.

I do hope that you make a swift recovery and may perhaps be able to return to work sooner than anticipated. You are already being missed by your colleagues, who also wish you well.

Yours sincerely

Ian Goodge
General Manager

IDENDEN INDUSTRIES
A division of Idenden Plc
Porter House, Hull HU7 4RF England

Tel 01482 119087 Fax 01482 119088
Registered in England No: 1218943

Mr P Townsend
56 Dockland Avenue
Hull
HU7 1KJ

1 July 1999

Mr Townsend,

Proposed Leave of Absence
I am in receipt of your letter requesting leave of absence with pay from 13 July to 14 July inclusive. In your letter you state your reasons as being that you are moving house.

You will be aware from your letter of appointment and from notices on the notice board, of the conditions under which leave of absence with pay are ordinarily granted. Moving house is not covered by these conditions and we regret, therefore, that we are unable to grant you leave of absence with pay.

In the circumstances, however, we are prepared to grant leave of absence for the two days in question, without pay, if this arrangement is acceptable to you.

Perhaps you would telephone my secretary as soon as possible to let me know what you decide.

Yours sincerely

J P Stone
Personnel Department

This is a formal letter from someone further up the line, who clearly has no day-to-day dealings with the employee. The tone is very impersonal and cold. Phrases such as "...I am in receipt of..." and "...You will be aware..." create this impression.

At the outset, one might imagine the letter to be uncompromising in its refusal. However, a solution is suggested which will probably be acceptable to the reader, in spite of being prefaced with a begrudging "In the circumstances...".

This letter is tricky because of the element of bad news that has to be given. The employee may already know what the rules are but, if she doesn't, she is likely to feel annoyed towards the company, even though the company is simply following the regulations as they stand.

Note how the writer tries to empathise with the employee's predicament: "I am sorry if you are disappointed..." and "We will do everything we can to help...". The writer also takes pains to explain that there is nothing he can do: "...you are not entitled by law..." and "We have no control over these regulations...", which should help to dissipate any anger that is felt towards the company.

Tyler & Piper Associates

76 Whites Lane, Stevenage, Herts SG1 8JP England
Tel: (01438) 186465 Fax: (01438) 164323

Mrs M Joseph
149 Bronsbury Park
Stevenage
Herts
SG1 7KJ

26 June 1999

Dear Mary,

Re: Statutory Maternity Pay
Firstly, Mary, I would like to say how delighted I am for you at your news – I do hope everything goes well for you.

As I mentioned to you, to qualify for statutory maternity pay you must have been continuously employed by us for at least 26 weeks, continuing into the 15th week before the week your baby is due.

Your expected week of confinement is the week commencing 16 October. Your qualifying week is the week commencing 3 July. To qualify for statutory maternity pay you would have had to commence your employment with us by 15 January. Unfortunately, because you did not join us until the 19 February you are not entitled by law to receive statutory maternity pay.

We have no control over these regulations and you will understand that, as a company, we are bound by them. However, I have discovered you will be able to claim maternity allowance. I will find out for you how to claim this allowance and the amount you will be entitled to receive.

I hope this clarifies the rules for you – I know it is not easy to take in when you haven't got the dates down on paper. I am sorry if you are disappointed to have missed the qualifying date by such a narrow margin. We will do everything we can to help and, if you would like to return to work following the birth of your child, we shall be delighted to welcome you back.

Yours sincerely

Harry Law
Personnel Manager

Partners: DA Tyler BA & SR Piper MA

Kelso Limited
16 Abbots Road, Luton, Bedford MK44 7YT
Tel: (01234) 136953 Fax: (01234) 136422
Registered in England No: 9126719 VAT No: 91523489 76

Peter Frost
45 Burgess Avenue
Luton
Bedford
MK43 8RE

13 August 1999

Dear Peter,

Thank you for sending your medical certificate to us, confirming that your doctor has advised you to rest for the next three weeks following your terrible bout of 'flu.

I am very sorry that this bug has hit you so hard. John and Harry have willingly stepped into the breach, to help out in the intervening period, so please don't worry about returning to a mountain of paper on your desk. They will try to confine it to a small hill and generally keep things ticking over until you return.

Put your feet up, drink plenty of fluids and get well soon.

Best wishes.

Yours sincerely

Charles Edwards
General Manager

Conscientious employees often feel badly about taking large amounts of time off, even when they are seriously unwell. It is important that the employee is not made to feel guilty about his illness. Coming back too early may only make matters worse.

This letter sets a reassuring tone and implies that everything is under control. A pleasantly informal note is struck by phrases like "...willingly stepped into the breach..." and "...will try to confine it to a small hill...".

The style of the last sentence is worth noting for other letters: the three instructions have a rhythmic flow that has a lot of impact, making for a memorable and impressive, yet friendly and informal, warm-hearted, close.

Sometimes, obstructive elements can reduce a person's ability to perform successfully.

Here, a manager is developing solutions to a problem that is preventing an employee from performing at his peak. Being seen to make these kinds of changes can go a long way to improving someone's morale. What might seem fairly trivial problems to the manager can appear as insuperable obstacles to the employee, particularly if the solution is beyond that person's control.

It is often worthwhile spending some time building your employee's confidence up again. This is achieved here in expressions such as: "You have a great deal to contribute..."; "I am confident....there will be considerable opportunities to increase your responsibilities" and "I know you will do your utmost...".

PARKER
Glass Ltd

Unit 27 Willow Park
Christchurch, Dorset BH23 6MM
Tel: 01202 109111
Fax: 01202 109112

Reg. No: England 962578762
VAT No: 9120564

Mr J Randall
Sales & Marketing Co-ordinator

22 February 1999

Dear John,

Thank you for being so frank and open about the difficulties that you have faced in the last few months. I hope that we may be able to reduce some of the conflicts that you have experienced and create a more fulfilling job for you. You have a great deal to contribute to the Sales and Marketing team and I am confident that, in the coming months, there will be considerable opportunities to increase your responsibilities.

In your role as Sales and Marketing Co-ordinator, you are, at present, reporting to two people: myself and the Sales Director. I recognise that this can create difficulties, especially when both of us demand a task to be performed at the same time and to the same deadline. From now on, you will report solely to me, and any tasks that the Sales Director requires will come through me. That way, I can monitor the flow of work and prevent one of the sources of conflict.

You should also not be afraid to raise problems (however minor) at an early stage with me. If you are not sure how to perform a particular task, or if there seem a number of ways for achieving the goal that has been given to you, please feel free to discuss them with me at any time. Two heads are often better than one, when it comes to solving difficult issues.

I agree that we should hold more regular feedback sessions and I suggest that we meet in a month's time, to review how the changes are working. Obviously, the prime issue is to achieve the sales targets that we have set ourselves. I know you will do your utmost to achieve the results we need.

Yours sincerely

T J Squires
Marketing Director

SIMPSON & MARTIN

39 TOP STREET
STOKE-ON-TRENT
ST2 3DR UNITED KINGDOM
Tel: (01782) 156232 Fax: (01782) 120899
Reg. No: England 96223978 VAT No: 91210674

Miss Karen Davis
Sales Administration

Dear Karen,

The strategy which we briefed you on this morning is the key to our success. If these targets are achieved, you can look forward to a bonus at the end of next year of over £1500. Now isn't that something worth working towards?

Do you remember how, three years ago, we were just one of many suppliers? While we have grown, our old competitors have shrunk away from us. Each one of you has made a marvellous contribution so far to the success of this company. But in every success story are the seeds of failure, and there is no room for complacency. We must be alert to new competitors and what they are doing. We must seize the opportunities that present themselves and make sure not one of them is missed. We must continue to talk to our customers and find out what our competitors are up to. If we are to be number one in three years time, we must have the resolve, guts, determination and drive to succeed.

We have a superb team, the goal is in view, and the foundations are laid. I know you can achieve what we are asking. All I ask is that you give it your all.

Yours sincerely

D B Fenton
Sales Director

This letter contains many of the ingredients of a successful motivational letter.

Using rhetorical questions helps to focus the mind on a particular point – here the bonus and how far the company has come in three years. It also deploys another tactic to engage people's interests – using 'we' and 'you' to focus attention on the audience and gain its commitment. If the letter had been peppered with many 'I's', the reader's attention would be focused more on the writer and its impact would be much reduced.

This letter brings out a horde of useful congratulatory phrases: "...prestigious award..."; "...wonderful achievement..." and "It means a great deal to me personally...".

The last sentence has a good ring to it, achieved by mirroring the first half of the sentence in the second half : "...and set the style for our age – a style which, I hope,..." – making it more memorable for the reader.

IDENDEN INDUSTRIES
A division of Idenden Plc
Porter House, Hull HU7 4RF England

Tel 01482 119087 Fax 01482 119088
Registered in England No: 1218943

Stephen Turner
Design Manager

27 May 1999

Dear Stephen,

Designer of the Year

I was delighted to hear you have won the designer of the year award for the best-produced annual report. Many congratulations.

This is the first time that someone from our firm has won this prestigious award and it is a wonderful achievement, both personally and professionally. I am doubly delighted because this award is a 'sock in the face' to our competitors, who have, for too long, been resting on their laurels. It means a great deal to me personally and to the firm. I am already looking forward to the many new clients who will be beating a path to our door.

Your designs have become a landmark for the industry, and set the style for our age – a style which, I hope, will continue for some time to come.

Yours sincerely

Ray Hooper
Technical Director

BELLS OF BASILDON

Bells of Basildon Ltd, Unit 12, Way Park, Basildon SS12 6DE
Tel: 01268 109 9954 Fax: 01268 109 5576 Reg. No. England 13078453 VAT No: 75698764

Mr R Norman
General Manager

13 December 1998

Dear Roy,

Holidays
We have decided to change the holiday policy of the company.

From 1 January 1999, all employees that have been with the company for five years will be entitled to an extra two days' holiday a year, in addition to their normal entitlement.

Those of you who have been with the company for less than five years, must serve a full five years by the 1 January to qualify for two extra days in that year. So, if your fifth anniversary arrives in June, you will not be entitled to take two extra days until the following 1 January.

I hope this clarifies the new policy but, if you have any queries, please do not hesitate to ask me personally.

Yours sincerely

David O'Brian
Director

With this kind of change, there are always going to be instant winners and those who will have to wait until they can benefit from the change. Introducing it has the twin benefit that it acts as a reward for those who have been with the company longer and as an incentive to stay for those who have not yet reached the date.

Letters of condolence are always difficult to write. No amount of words can help to replace the loss. All that can be hoped for is that the small words of comfort will help to alleviate the grief.

The letter wants to be brief and, above all, sincere. If you can say a few personal words of tribute to the departed person or remember some of his or her characteristics, this will help to lift the letter, increase the impact of your message and be appreciated by the grieving relative.

Hart & Tucker Ltd

19 Green Street, Maidstone, Kent ME41 1TJ
Telephone: (01622) 109109
Facsimile: (01622) 108106
Reg. No: England 96223978 VAT No: 91210674

Mrs P Burnett
35 Masons Avenue
Maidstone
Kent
ME41 7UJ

16 August 1999

Dear Mrs Burnett

I was very sorry to hear your sad news.

Although I only knew Alex briefly, I thoroughly enjoyed working with him and found his professionalism and dedication to his consultancy second to none. When Alex broke the news to me of his cancer, I was amazed at the way he was able to continue working, providing answers to our enquiries and checking details throughout the project and, true to his dedication, always keeping to the time-scales that were requested.

The successful completion of the project gave Alex a great sense of pride and I hope it will be a source of comfort to you to know that, as a tribute to him, we would like to name the last building which he designed the Alex Burnett Building. I hope it will be a source of comfort to know that Alex's work will be remembered in this way.

Please accept the most sincere condolences and deepest sympathy, from all at Hart & Tucker Ltd.

Yours sincerely

J P Smith
Managing Director

Thomas King & Palmer Ltd

serving the world

24 Fuller Road, Welling,
Kent DA16 7JP
Tel : (01322) 100132
Fax : (01322) 100178

Reg. No : England 1212298762
VAT No : 92905643

Mr & Mrs P Strong
34 Kelvin Drive
Welling
Kent
DA16 5GP

26 September 1999

Dear Mr and Mrs Strong,

We were deeply shocked by John's untimely death and I am writing to extend our heartfelt condolences to you both at this painful time.

John was an outstanding member of his team and an extremely loyal and conscientious employee. He always went about his work so willingly and cheerfully and it will be very difficult for us to forget his bubbly personality, which lifted everyone's spirits so much. We will miss him sorely.

Please accept our sincere sympathy on your loss. If there is anything we can do, please let us know.

Yours sincerely

Andrew Rogers
Managing Director

A sudden and tragic death can make the task of writing a condolence letter all the more difficult. The opening sentence here is a good one to use, when a letter like this is required. It has the right mix of empathy and sincerity, even though the level of shock felt by the writer will always be less than the grieving relative.

The rule of being brief and sincere still applies. Note the clutch of phrases that can be used for similar condolence letters: "We were deeply shocked…"; "…it will be very difficult for us to forget…"; "We will miss him sorely" and "Please accept our sincere sympathy…".

CHAPTER FIVE

Sales and Marketing Management

Writing a really good sales letter that persuades customers to buy your product is one of the toughest assignments. You need to have an ear, not only for your product or service, but also for what makes your customers place their orders. Letters associated with other forms of selling are depicted (for example, through agencies and distributors), as well as responses to the media for information and dealings with advertising agencies.

Letters that sell

Seven letters that are designed to sell a product or service are given here (letters 70–6). Each one takes a slightly different standpoint and picks a different approach for getting through to the customer. You have to accept that you won't get through to everyone; it's all a question of which one produces the biggest response.

Letters to agents and distributors

Handling agents is a skill of its own and operating at a distance raises the importance of letters and faxes in maintaining the lines of communications. As letters 77–84 show, many different types have to be written to agents, from simple responses to letters of thanks, reprimands and complaints, each one requiring a different tone.

Advertising agencies

When dealing with advertising agencies, a tough line is needed to make sure they stick to your instructions and don't try to get off the hook when matters don't go to plan. The secret to making sure everything goes smoothly is having instructions firmly in writing.

'Just imagine..." is a useful tactic which can be used to plant the reader into imaginary situations as here: "Wouldn't you love to be a fly on the wall of your competitors...".

Note how the letter reserves underlining for the financial benefits of the service. The eye is drawn to this part of the letter first and, with the interest aroused, you are encouraged to read the complete letter.

Brendall Thomas Consultancy

Bringing Business to Business

65 Brentwood Road
Sheffield
South Yorkshire
S18 2JP
Tel: (0114) 200132
Fax: (0114) 200178

Reg No: England 1298762122
VAT No: 56439290

16 May 1999

Dear Business Manager

Wouldn't you love to be a fly on the walls of your competitors, finding out how they operate?

Just imagine finding out what the secrets of their success are – how they manage to do things faster and smarter? But why turn to your competitors? There are simply dozens of organisations with whom you don't compete who are willing to share their secrets with you. Secrets which could, quite literally, <u>save you thousands of pounds</u>. How?

They have discovered, through sheer hard work and experimentation, different and better ways of operating. Ways that they can pass on to you and which will have tangible results for your business. And why should they be interested in sharing their secrets with you? Because you will also have different ways of operating which will be of interest to them. It all works on the time-honoured principle of 'if you scratch my back, I'll scratch yours'.

This system, which you may know as 'benchmarking', has worked for literally hundreds of companies world-wide. At the Brendall Thomas Consultancy, we have the contacts and experience to match your business up with another like-minded firm. Step by step, we guide you through a systematic benchmarking programme that is specifically designed to deliver tangible results. Bottom-line results which will far exceed the cost to your business of implementing the programme. <u>One company found that by restructuring their despatch services they were able to save over £10,000 per annum.</u>

To find out how our benchmarking programme will improve your bottom line, call me now on (0114) 200132.

Yours sincerely

Simon Framlington
Brendall Thomas Consultancy

PS. Remember, our results are guaranteed!

RPP Holdings Plc
35/38 New Road, Paignton, Devon TQ3 4UU
Tel: 01803 175653 Fax: 01803 187908
Reg. No: England 1976143

Mr J Cox
56 Brighton Road
Reading
Berkshire
RG2 6GF

16 June 1999

Dear Investor,

If you had invested £2000 in Yossiver shares in January, today they would be worth £9500. However, an investment of £2000 in Yossiver warrants in the same period would have been worth over £98,000 – a rise in excess of 4,800%!

Warrants are one of the most exciting investment opportunities available. But be warned. They are not for the faint-hearted. Without professional guidance, it is very easy to go astray. While we can guarantee that you will have an exciting time seeing some really spectacular gains, at the same time, we recommend that you hold a mixed portfolio to cushion the downside. However, our performance to date is excellent, with an average per annum return for our clients of 35%.

Now you, too, can enjoy these returns at special preferential rates to readers of Investment Today. For a limited period, if you have £5000 or more to invest, you can take advantage of our private client expertise, for a fixed fee of £100 and 1 per cent of the cost of transactions to buy warrants and 2 per cent of the cost of selling transactions.

For this special rate we will :

- Structure a balanced portfolio to suit your needs.
- Provide expert guidance on the performance of warrants.
- Advise on new exciting opportunities.
- Handle all the documentation on your behalf.

Whether you are a seasoned investor or would just like to dip your toe into the market for the first time, call me now on 01803 175653, for a confidential discussion about how we can open up these opportunities to you.

Yours sincerely

Tony Granger
Marketing Manager

PS. Call me now, even if you may not be interested until later.

Using the lure of what might have been 'if only' is a handy way of attracting interest, especially where the gain is spectacular. Here it is used as an attention grabber, even though the letter goes on to mention a much more modest performance.

Tying up with another organisation to create a 'special offer' is another trick to catch people's interest. Note how the telephone number is referred to in the text, to make it easier for people to contact the writer, and how the PS urges you to call him now, even if you may only be interested later. This aims to catch a wider audience than might otherwise be reached.

This is a useful sales technique when you are trying to sell something which the customer cannot see. People are naturally reluctant to subscribe to a service unseen. Getting the product in front of the potential customer increases confidence and the propensity to buy.

Incentives are also used to increase the desire for the product. Note also the tone used in this letter – it is very confident, which, combined with its enthusiasm for the product, should engender customer-confidence in the product.

SIMPSON & MARTIN

39 TOP STREET
STOKE-ON-TRENT
ST2 3DR UNITED KINGDOM
Tel: (01782) 156232 Fax: (01782) 120899
Reg. No: England 96223978 VAT No: 91210674

22 January 1999

Dear Business Manager,

The best way to tell you about **Business Now** is <u>to show it to you</u>. So here, with my compliments, is an issue for you to see.

Business Now is packed with practical advice for busy managers. It's brief, succinct and to the point. It delivers tried and tested techniques and shortcuts *that work*. To save you time, money and hassle again and again.

It's published every fortnight; sifting and distilling the latest ideas from the ever-growing mountain of management publications and seminars available. Covering just about every aspect of your work as a manager of time, people and resources.

There's no waffle ... no padding ... no advertisements.

Just practical, valuable tips and tactics that you can lift right off the page and put to work in your job. And it's delivered direct to your desk every two weeks, 24 issues a year.

Take a look yourself – I'm sure you'll find some ideas in this issue that you can use at once.

What's more, join now and we will send you **absolutely FREE (a saving of £19.95), Dirty Negotiating Tactics and their solutions,** one of the most popular reports ever produced, which exposes 39 underhand tactics that suppliers may try to use against you while negotiating. We expose every one – and show you how to counter them.

I've also enclosed a copy of the latest Business Now index – listing hundreds of different topics Business Now has tackled over the last six months. I'm certain you'll find it packed with articles that will interest you.

To get your own, regular issue of Business Now, simply fax back the yellow order form enclosed on 01782 120899. I look forward to welcoming you as a subscriber.

Yours sincerely

Andrew Clifford
Marketing Manager

PS Reply before 30 November and we'll also send you a superb compact calculator <u>in addition to</u> your Special Bonus Report worth £19.95. So hurry – fax me now!

⊛ WILSON SMITH LTD

A wholly-owned subsidiary of The Wilson Group PLC
16 Willow Walk, Retford, Nottingham NG6 8WS
Tel: (01777) 121211 Fax: (01777) 121233
Reg. No: England 1212298762

Mrs M Catt
Despatch Manager
Elba-Ross Limited
4 The Business Park
Nottingham
NG1 4TL

12 February 1999

Dear Mrs Catt,

Twelve months ago Sam was starting out in business – a direct mail business supplying gardening products direct to end-users.

In the first six months, everything appeared to be going well. Responses to his advertisements were increasing week by week and orders were 15% ahead of his business plan.

But, unfortunately for Sam, everything was not so lovely in the garden.

For his business to grow, Sam depended on a lot of repeat business to help cover the high cost of advertising in glossy gardening magazines. Sadly, Sam was not getting the repeat business he needed, to stay in business. At first, it was not clear what was going wrong. The product range gave customers just what they needed, at a price that was competitive, and the customer service was second to none. It was only after Sam carried out a customer questionnaire that things started to fall into place.

The replies to the questionnaire confirmed that the products were fine, the prices good and the customer service was excellent. But what was being kept hidden from Sam was the delivery service he was receiving. His customers felt they were having to wait just too long to receive the goods. So, instead of coming back to him, they preferred to whizz down to the garden centre to get what they needed.

Sam immediately sacked the courier service he had been using and, after contacting a friend who had some experience, he chose Wilson Smith, because we were the only courier service who both <u>guaranteed delivery and promised that, if he failed to deliver on time, we would reimburse him with any income which he lost as a result of the late delivery</u>. As you can imagine, this helps Sam sleep at night and it gives us just a small incentive to get the goods there on time. Sam is now happy to report that his customers are coming back in droves.

So, if you would like to join Sam in helping your business to thrive and grow, take a look at Wilson Smith – the professionals' choice – for professionals. Call us now on (01777) 121 211.

Yours sincerely

Tony Milner
Manager

PS If you agree to sign up for a trial period before the 30 March, we will give you half-price deliveries for a week!

It's not just letters with an emotional appeal that can successfully use the story-telling approach, as this letter demonstrates. The interesting thing about the story style is that you are not aware of what is being offered until you are well into the letter. The story has been used to attract your interest – you want to know what happens to Sam.

The drawback, of which you should be aware, is that some readers may be disappointed when they find out that it is just a run-of-the-mill courier-service operation that is being offered. Nevertheless, the message has got through – and in a more interesting way than in many conventional sales letters.

If you make people curious, they will want to know more. This sales letter is unusual in that the nature of the business is kept secret. To find out more, you have to buy the book. There is a money-back guarantee, so customers will have nothing to lose.

It also uses the technique of painting an attractive image that assumes you have already put the plan into action and reaped the results – which is often the hardest part of all – yet it makes it sound so easy – you don't need much money or time.

Note how it also succeeds in overcoming many objections and suspicions that people may harbour: "If it is so great why give the secret away?".

Grange & Turner Ltd

32 WESTBOURN ROAD, WITNEY, OXON OX6 7HY

Telephone (01993) 107888
Fax (01993) 107843

Reg. No: England 13078453
VAT No: 75698764

Mr A C R Lloyd
3 Black Horse Lane
Kings Heath
Birmingham
B14 5TG

14 February 1999

Dear Mr Lloyd,

Would you like to earn over £15,000 by working in your spare time from home? Or much more if you work longer? This plan shows you precisely how to do it.

The only premises you need – your home. The only start-up money – £500. The only time you need (once the business is set up and running) is around two hours a day telling others what to do.

Is this just an unproven idea? No! This plan gives you full details of a specific business.

It tells you how to set it up. Where to buy your supplies. Who to go to for help. It names names. It shows you how to find others to do the selling required for you – and why you should not do it yourself. It shows you why no experience is necessary – indeed previous experience has been found to be a real disadvantage.

And above all it works! There are already people up and down the country making money from this type of business. For example, there is an ex-sales manager for a car manufacturer. He started this business ten years ago when the author introduced him to the idea. He has been making good money ever since.

So why haven't I told you what this business is about? The answer is that it needs a full description before you can fairly judge. Since I heard about this business and read the book I have told many friends about it. As soon as I outline the business they automatically bring all their preconceived notions to bear. They at once think of other businesses which at first sight appear very similar – businesses which are not outstandingly profitable and which really do need great expertise.

It is not until I have had the chance to describe the whole plan in detail that these initial negatives are cleared away. Then it becomes clear just how great an opportunity for money-making it is. And that no experience at all is a positive advantage – because there is no tendency to tinker with the system to make 'improvements'.

If it is so great why give the secret away? Well, this is the sort of business which could be set up anywhere. There is room for thousands up and down the country – so the author loses nothing by offering his secret.

Sounds too good to be true? Judge for yourself, it is on 10 days free approval. So you can delve into the programme as soon as you receive it and weigh it up for yourself. When you have read this book from cover to cover you too will be convinced that the plan does work.

Yours sincerely

J P Parsons
Marketing Director

PS Do you want to get rich? Are you prepared to take risks?

IDENDEN INDUSTRIES
A division of Idenden Plc
Porter House, Hull HU7 4RF England

Tel 01482 119087 Fax 01482 119088
Registered in England No: 1218943

Mr A Begoyu
Managing Director
News Today – Teban Kian Pte Ltd
BLK 31 Heng Gardens Road,
Tampines Industrial Park
5100 Kuala Lumpar
Malaysia

16 February 1999

Dear Mr Begoyu

I have been advised by John Williams of Newspaper Supplies Limited that you may be interested in web offset news black.

We have in the past supplied New Independent as well as many other newspapers in Malaysia and, therefore, we feel fully confident that our product will be suitable for your requirements. I believe that we can offer competitive prices at £1.10 per kg C & F for 11,000kg and approximately £1.06 per kg for 15,000kg. If you find this of interest, please advise and we will send to you the necessary pro forma invoices.

I enclose our brochure, outlining some of the major products which we are able to supply. You may also be interested to learn that we have recently obtained the Agency for Malaysia from the company who have taken over from Hill & Webb, to manufacture gravure ink. If, therefore, you require any prices for cigarette carton inks which were previously supplied by Hill & Webb, we will be happy to quote for these.

I look forward to hearing from you with regard to any of our printing products.

Yours sincerely,

Richard Russell
International Sales Director

If you offer a product to someone with whom you have had no personal dealings before, you have, at first, nothing in common. You are often left searching around for points of mutual interest.

The pain of searching for that common ground can be reduced if you are able to demonstrate a mutual acquaintance. It does, at least, give you a topic of conversation to build upon, and is considerably easier than appearing to be just another salesperson on the make. If you can get referrals like this, seize them.

This is a good letter to write when making an approach to a company out of the blue.

It doesn't pressurise the customer at all. It sets out the services on offer clearly and concisely and uses the company brochure that had been left earlier as an excuse for following up the enquiry.

It also highlights the benefits that many businesses may not automatically think about: that wasted space may be costing them more than they think.

GKT Products Ltd, Unit 10, Castleway Lane, Alloway, Ayr, KA7 4BE
Telephone (01292) 177900 Fax (01292) 199855   Reg. No: 17964583 VAT No: 679845

Mrs N Hall
Purchasing Manager
Johnson & Cole Ltd
226 Mill Road
Hawick
Roxboroughshire
TD9 8UK

16 April 1999

Dear Mrs Hall,

On a recent visit to your company, I left for your attention our company brochure, and this letter is to outline our service, which may be of interest to you.

GKT Products Ltd specialise in the design, supply and installation of commercial and industrial partitioning, suspended ceilings, raised-access flooring and mezzanine storage platforms. We also supply and install all types of shelving and racking, as authorised distributors for the major manufacturers. We can, therefore, offer a complete and comprehensive service should you be considering, now, or in the future, developing your existing facility.

Many companies have benefited from our expertise in assisting with re-design of office and factory space, and making the best use of wasted space, which, is, invariably, costing money.

We fully understand that, in the current economic climate, expenditure on these items may not be a priority but, with the benefit of professional advice, it is possible to make savings by careful planning and design. As licensed credit brokers, we can also offer a full leasing service on our products. By taking advantage of this, you can spread payment over varying terms to suit your budget; cash-flow is protected by not having to pay fully upon completion of the work, and leasing is subject to 100% tax relief.

If you are interested in our services, for current or future purposes, please do not hesitate to contact us. We will provide, absolutely free of charge and without obligation, detailed costings and designs to assist you in your future planning.

If, for some reason, you did not receive our brochure, please let me know and one will be sent to you without delay. I look forward to hearing from you.

Yours sincerely

Garry Stream
Sales Manager

IDENDEN INDUSTRIES
A division of Idenden Plc
Porter House, Hull HU7 4RF England

Tel 01482 119087 Fax 01482 119088
Registered in England No: 1218943

Tony Fuller
Marketing Manager
BSG Ltd
19 West Walk
Wallsend
Tyne & Wear
NE28 7DF

16 March 1999

Dear Tony,

Thank you for your letter dated 10th August, regarding
Idenden Seal distribution for Europe.

Currently, Morplan are distributing this product for us in Europe
and we are presently discussing a sole agency deal with them.
In the circumstances, I must turn down your request. If you
consider the opportunity for the Idenden Seal in Europe is
important to you, I am sure Morplan would be pleased to
supply you with stocks.

Thank you for your interest in our range of products.

Yours sincerely,

Peter Collins
Marketing Director

The company here could have decided to play one company off against the other, to negotiate the best deal for itself. It has, though, developed considerable goodwill and trust with Morplan, who it finds satisfactory. It is therefore unwilling to jeopardise that relationship and decides to decline the other offer. Note how it makes a positive suggestion with the line "...I am sure Morplan would be pleased to supply you with stocks".

It is important that you engage in a formal agreement with an agent or distributor. This letter precedes the agreement and outline the terms and procedures governing the agency.

It serves the purpose of pre-empting awkward issues that may have been overlooked or misunderstood in the course of discussions and still need to be ironed out.

The layout is clear and numbering paragraphs gives the recipient a reference point, if he needs to refer to it in a reply.

IDENDEN INDUSTRIES
A division of Idenden Plc
Porter House, Hull HU7 4RF England

Tel 01482 119087 Fax 01482 119088
Registered in England No: 1218943

Herr Gunter Mann
Stepham Meins and Co
Burgstr 18
D-87600 Kaufbeuren
Germany

7 January 1999

Dear Gunter,

Agency – North Western Europe
I am pleased to confirm your appointment as agent for North Western Europe. A formal contract will be drawn up this week but I would like to clarify the main points that we agreed.

1. **Period of appointment**. Your appointment will be for an initial trial period of four months. At the end of the trial period, we shall review the performance of the agency. Thereafter, if either party wishes to terminate the agency, three months' notice must be given in writing to the other side, subject to issues regarding the solvency of either party, which will be specified in the formal agreement.

2. **Territory.** The territory of your agency will be North Western Europe. This will include, specifically, the countries of: Belgium, Netherlands, Luxembourg, Germany, and Switzerland. We will not appoint any other agents to these countries during the term of our agreement.

3. **Targets**. You will achieve a minimum sales target within the first year of £500,000 of business. If this target is not met, we reserve the right to terminate the agency. The target will be reviewed on 1 January each year. If a new target is not agreed by either party, the new target that will apply will be the current target plus 5 per cent.

4. **Commission**. You will be paid by commission only and receive 10 per cent of the invoiced value of the goods sold by your agency. All credit notes issued in respect of invoices will be deducted from the invoiced value, for the purposes of calculating the commission. With the following exceptions, all costs and expenses will be borne by your agency:
   - Travel to and from the United Kingdom at the company's

request.
- Accommodation expenses for overnight stays in the United Kingdom required by the company.

5. **Procedure and payment**. We will send you a copy of all purchase orders received and invoices issued for sales made in your territory. At the end of each month, you will send us a statement of the commission which is owing on sales made within the calendar month, quoting the correct invoice number, invoice total and commission claimed. We will pay your statement within ten days of its receipt.

6. **Representation.** All representations that you make to customers will be within the guidelines laid down in our conditions of sale. You will not have any right to negotiate terms outside our normal, standard terms without the written permission of the Sales Manager. You will not have the right to enter into any contract in our name. All contracts with customers will be between the company and the customer. You will not, during the period of this agency, represent any of our competitors or any product which competes with the sales of our products.

7. **Law.** Our agreement will be made under English law.

This covers the main points of our agreement. A detailed contract will be drawn up within the week but, if you have any queries or concerns about any of the items confirmed, please let me know as soon as possible.

Yours sincerely

Bill Tanner
European Marketing Director

This is a straightforward thank-you letter for some business that has been obtained. These kinds of letters help to build goodwill amongst business colleagues and encourage further deals. It costs nothing to say: "Thank you for your time and effort on our behalf" and "Thank you again for your assistance..." but it can be worth more than the 10 per cent commission that has been paid here.

GKT Products Ltd, Unit 10, Castleway Lane, Alloway, Ayr, KA7 4BE
Telephone (01292) 177900 Fax (01292) 199855 Reg. No: 17964583 VAT No: 679845

Ms Claire Norman
Tuttle & Parkin Ltd
29 High Road West
Stranraer
DG9 7TG

13 December 1998

Dear Claire,

It was a pleasure to meet with you at Falkirk Fashions just prior to Christmas and we are pleased to advise you that Mr Fitzsimmons has ordered one of the bottom-seal units - unfortunately we missed out on two units. However it is good to get one. Thank you for your time and effort on our behalf.

We hope to deliver the unit during the first week of February and, we hope, those of Mr Fitzsimmons colleagues in the clothing industry who use sellotape to close bags might also be interested, if Mr Fitzsimmons' bottom-seal unit proves to be a success.

As mentioned to you prior to our visit, we will reserve you a commission of 10% against this sale.

Thank you again for your assistance and all good wishes for a successful 1999.

Yours sincerely,

Paul Fisher
Marketing Manager

IDENDEN INDUSTRIES
A division of Idenden Plc
Porter House, Hull HU7 4RF England

Tel 01482 119087 Fax 01482 119088
Registered in England No: 1218943

Pierre Balan
Director General
Roodebeek Associates
Ev Swedenlann 7
B-2100 Brussels
Belgium

11 November 1999

Dear Pierre,

Re: Hermanns of Hannover
We have been contacted by Hermanns of Hannover, with regard to the discount given on their latest invoice. This was for a batch of items which you had sold to them on your last visit. Their complaint is that they have not received the special discount which was promised when you sold the goods to them. They have supported their claim with a copy of a fax from you, which confirms your agreement to increase the discount to them by 10 per cent. This is enclosed.

Our agreement expressly forbids you to negotiate discount terms unless they have been otherwise agreed in writing between us, prior to discussing them with the customer. You have not had the authority to grant an extra discount and, furthermore, your failure to notify us of your agreement has caused us considerable embarrassment with what is one of our most important European customers. It also nearly jeopardised our relations with them, since they were expecting to receive this additional discount not only on this order but also on all future orders as well. Fortunately, they have been understanding on the issue and, while we have agreed to the extra discount on this invoice, our terms will revert to the original discount agreed on all future business placed by them.

Your conduct in this matter has been extremely disappointing and, if a we are to continue with your agency, you must, in future, adhere strictly to the letter of our agreement. We are prepared to give you another chance but, if there is another serious breach, we shall have no option but to terminate the agreement.

Yours sincerely

Bill Tanner
European Marketing Director

If the mark has been overstepped, a severe rap on the knuckles is called for, to bring an agent back into line.

Note how the severity of the tone develops over successive phrases: "Our agreement expressly forbids you..."; "You have not had the authority..."; "...your failure to notify us..."; "...caused us considerable embarrassment..."; "...nearly jeopardised our relations...". And rises to a crescendo in the final paragraph: "Your conduct in this matter has been extremely disappointing..."; "...you must, in future, adhere strictly..." and "...we shall have no option but to terminate...".

The letter conveys the depth of the writer's feelings, but, despite its sternness, retains a calm tone.

When such a stern reprimand has been received and the accusations are completely erroneous, the denial must be equally strong to carry sufficient weight. This is achieved with a series of firm phrases: "I was very disturbed..."; "...I wish to deny in the strongest terms possible..."; "I am well aware of the restrictions to which I am bound..." and "...would not dream of stepping beyond the powers...".

Roodebeek Associates

Roodebeek Associates
Ev Swedenlann 7
B-2100 Brussels
Belgium
Tel: 2 7567001
Fax: 2 7569400

Bill Tanner
European Marketing Director
Idenden Industries
Porter House
Hull
HU7 4RF
England

24 November 1999

Dear Bill,

Re: Hermanns of Hannover
I was very disturbed to receive your letter concerning Hermanns account.

Firstly, I wish to deny in the strongest terms possible that I ever consented to giving them an additional 10 per cent discount. It is true that their previous buyer, who was there for only two months, had requested more discount from me but I refused to budge on the issue, referring him to yourself.

The fax which you copied to me is a forgery. I have never written such a letter. I am well aware of the restrictions to which I am bound in my agreement with you and would not dream of stepping beyond the powers which you have granted to me. If you compare the signature with my own, I think you will realise how different the two are. The typeface is also not one which I use in my correspondence.

I understand the buyer with whom I dealt was subsequently sacked for theft and incompetence, just two months after he had been appointed to the position. I can only imagine that it was this buyer who perpetrated this deception out of spite, and that fax has lain dormant in the file, before being discovered by the new buyer.

I will aim to arrange a meeting next week with their new buyer to discuss this matter, which is as disturbing to me as it is to you.

Yours sincerely

Pierre Balan
Director General

Roodebeek Associates

Roodebeek Associates
Ev Swedenlann 7
B-2100 Brussels
Belgium
Tel: 2 7567001
Fax: 2 7569400

Bill Tanner
European Marketing Director
Idenden Industries
Porter House
Hull
HU7 4RF
England

12 June 1999

Dear Bill,

Re: Prices in Europe
Thanks for sending through the latest price changes.

Now that we have been running your agency in Europe for three months, I wanted to discuss some difficulties that our team are experiencing in some local markets. Unfortunately, we have discovered more resistance than we initially anticipated to stocking your range of gift products. The main objection we are finding is that your prices are too high and uncompetitive compared with the alternative ranges that are available. Frankly, we are losing out on bulk orders, which I know we could secure if only we were able to price according to local market needs. I am confident that if your European prices were reduced by 15 per cent we could achieve 30 per cent more sales.

Could we discuss this when I come over to the UK next week?

Yours sincerely

Pierre Balan
Director General

You should always remember that agents have a lot more to offer than simply to generate sales. Being on the ground gives them a unique perspective on the market. They are far closer to customers than anyone in a head office and will be able to judge more easily how they are reacting to the products on offer.

Here, the agent is giving some feedback about prices, based on the experience of three months in the market with their product. He is trying to persuade them that a different pricing regime needs to be considered for the mainland European market.

The company has to decide which part of the market they want to be in, and if they should alter their prices accordingly.

The company responds with a reaffirmation of the market that it is trying to reach. The tone of the letter is questioning, particularly the penultimate paragraph, which picks out a number of issues that need to be talked through. Asking a series of questions like this is a good tactic to use if you want to stall or slow down the progress of a project.

IDENDEN INDUSTRIES
A division of Idenden Plc
Porter House, Hull HU7 4RF England

Tel 01482 119087 Fax 01482 119088
Registered in England No: 1218943

Pierre Balan
Director General
Roodebeek Associates
Ev Swedenlann 7
B-2100 Brussels
Belgium

19 June 1999

Dear Pierre,

Re: Prices in Europe
Many thanks for your letter of 12 June about the price of our products in Europe.

As I am sure you are aware, the costs of servicing European orders is substantially more compared with UK orders and I am reluctant to take any action that is going to erode our margins. Before we make any decision about establishing a local European price, I would like my reservations to be satisfied.

As you know, we never anticipated taking a share of the mass market in Europe for gift ware. Our strategy with the product has always been to focus on the quality end of the market. I wonder if your team are attempting to take it into outlets for which it was never really intended? I think we need to review urgently the way the product is being sold.

Could you also be specific about the competition we are up against? I think we need real examples to analyse the position. Can you supply brochures of the competition's products? Although you are confident about increasing sales by 30 per cent with a 15 per cent drop in prices, what about the higher level of returns that we would have to accept? Have you costed this into your assessment?

I agree we should discuss this when you come over next week and I will put it at the top of our agenda.

Yours sincerely

Bill Tanner
European Marketing Director

B & R HENDERSONS LTD
Marlows Road, Aberdeen AB20 5GT
Tel: 01224 267855 Fax: 01224 267977
Reg. No: 16497811 VAT No: 7387945

Barry Hall
Marketing Manager
Hart & Tucker Ltd
19 Green Street
Maidstone
Kent
ME41 1TJ

20 August 1999

Dear Barry,

Re: Price Review
We have reviewed the price changes to our products for the next 12 months. Enclosed with this letter is a copy of the price list, with the revisions which will take effect from 1 September.

When making our review, we looked critically at our competitors' prices in the market as well as our own pricing strategy. I am delighted to say that our strategy of providing a superb range of affordable products with a perceived higher added-value than our competitors remains unchanged. We have striven to keep the price increases to an absolute inflation-only minimum, although a few of the products which are not so price-sensitive are increasing by around 10%. These are the premier brands in their field and we are confident the market for them will not be adversely affected.

We would obviously be interested in any feedback on these price changes that you receive from customers. And, don't forget, you are welcome to negotiate special discounts within the company's guidelines.

Yours sincerely

Brian Henderson
Marketing Director

Selling a price increase to agents can be as difficult as selling a price increase to customers. Anything that gets in the way of maximising sales will find resistance.

The company here tries to counter any resistance to a price increase by emphasising that they are concerned to offer "...affordable products with a perceived higher added-value..." coupled with the news that they have "...striven to keep the price increases to an absolute inflation-only minimum...".

Expressions of confidence that "...the market for them will not be adversely affected" with the reminder that they can "...negotiate special discounts..." should help to offset any concern the agents may feel.

This letter appears to adopt an open attitude towards the newspaper. It admits that a person is leaving the company and accepts that there were differences about the future direction of the business.

But it successfully covers up any notion that the parting is not amicable on both sides, by expressing sorrow at losing the person and confirming that his departure is "...entirely voluntary...". It also uses the opportunity to give an optimistic impression about the company's future, for which there are "...new and exciting opportunities", without giving anything tangible away.

Thomas King & Palmer Ltd

serving the world

24 Fuller Road, Welling,
Kent DA16 7JP
Tel : (01322) 100132
Fax : (01322) 100178

Reg. No : England 1212298762
VAT No : 92905643

The Editor
Attica Magazine
27 Mason Street
London
N1P 4KK

13 March 1999

Dear Sir/Madam

Thank you for your request for a comment on the departure of our Managing Director, John Roberts.

We are all very sorry to be losing John so unexpectedly, especially as he has committed such a large part of his career to us. I would like to make clear that, although we had our differences on the future direction of the business, John's decision to leave was entirely voluntary. He has made a brilliant contribution to the business both here and internationally and he has a superb record of achievement, which I am confident will stand him in good stead for the future.

However, I believe the change will be mutually beneficial. It is true that the company is experiencing upheaval as it responds to the challenges we face in our industry, but we have a major investment programme under way and we are creating new and exciting opportunities, which will reap rewards for us in the future. In addition, we have recently reorganised our management structure to allow our operating executives a greater degree of autonomy.

I will be taking over John's duties for the foreseeable future, until a successor is appointed.

Yours sincerely

Peter Abraham
Chairman

BELLS OF BASILDON

Bells of Basildon Ltd, Unit 12, Way Park, Basildon SS12 6DE
Tel: 01268 109 9954 Fax: 01268 109 5576 Reg. No. England 13078453 VAT No: 75698764

Peter White
PIR Media Direct
38 St Marys Street
London
E9 5TG

17 June 1999

Dear Peter,

This is to confirm the details and the key terms of the offer we have accepted for advertising space.

Medium: **It Magazine**
Issue date: **02.07.99**
Copy date: **27.06.99**
Gross cost: **£2400**
Media discount: **15%**
Space and agreed position: **Full-Page, Right-Hand, Front-Half**
Key Code: **UH9**

1.   Position.
The position is an integral part of this deal. No deviation is acceptable, except where this has been specifically agreed in writing by us before the copy date. Otherwise, if a change in position becomes inevitable, the advertisement MUST NOT BE RUN. Where an advertisement is run in the wrong position, any payment will be entirely at our discretion, and will normally be in the range of 10% to 50% of the above price, depending on the degree of variation from the agreed position.

2.   Payment.
Payment falls due on the 28th of the month following insertion. Payment on any advertisement under dispute will be withheld until a satisfactory outcome has been negotiated by your agency with the media owner.

Yours sincerely

Rita Smith
Marketing Production Manager

When dealing with an advertising agency that is in turn placing an advertisement on your behalf in a magazine, there is scope for mistakes to occur as messages get passed down the chain of command. If the company is not careful, the agency may blame mistakes on the magazine, while the magazine blames the agency for not giving proper instructions.

Spelling out the terms in a tough manner, when placing the business through the agency, will prevent a lot of arguments later on.

93

The position of an advertisement in a magazine can affect the response that is received. The position was crucial to the company placing it and an express part of the agreement.

This letter is a firm and abrupt rebuttal to the agency, spelling out that the agreed rate will not be paid. It is written with the negotiating strength of the agreed terms and conditions. Note the forceful tone that several of the phrases give: "...on the strict understanding..."; "...we are exercising our right not to pay..."; "...we will not pay any more..." and "I hope this makes our position clear".

BELLS OF BASILDON

Bells of Basildon Ltd, Unit 12, Way Park, Basildon SS12 6DE
Tel: 01268 109 9954 Fax: 01268 109 5576 Reg. No. England 13078453 VAT No: 75698764

Peter White
PIR Media Direct
38 St Marys Street
London
E9 5TG

6 July 1999

Dear Peter,

IT Magazine advertisement

As you know, the advertisement which went in 'IT' magazine on the 2 July issue was placed on the strict understanding that it would appear on a Right-Hand, Front-Half position. This position is crucial to us if the response that we predict is not to be depressed.

The advertisement we placed appeared on page 53, a left-hand page which is three quarters of the way through the magazine. Under the terms on which our order was placed, we are exercising our right not to pay the agreed rate. In the circumstances, we will not pay any more than 30 per cent of the agreed price for the advertisement.

I hope this makes our position clear. On this understanding, please negotiate a revised rate with the magazine.

Yours sincerely

Rita Smith
Marketing Production Manager

BELLS OF BASILDON

Bells of Basildon Ltd, Unit 12, Way Park, Basildon SS12 6DE
Tel: 01268 109 9954 Fax: 01268 109 5576 Reg. No. England 13078453 VAT No: 75698764

Peter White
PIR Media Direct
38 St Marys Street
London
E9 5TG

17 August 1999

Dear Peter,

Thanks for looking into the possibility of arranging last-minute advertising deals in World magazine and Attica.

It is disappointing that Attica don't go in for distress space, but thanks for trying. The rate of £4995 is just too much for us to be able to justify, bearing in mind the response that we have obtained from our entry last year.

World magazine's rate of £4500 is better and we just about broke even on the last advertisement we ran with them. I am willing to give the 28 October issue another try, provided we can obtain a front-half position that faces editorial for this same rate. We will get copy organised by the deadline of 21 October.

Yours sincerely

Paula Little
Advertising Manager

Getting hold of distress space (low-cost advertising space which a magazine is desperate to fill) can be a very cost-effective way of advertising.

You have to be prepared to be flexible about when your advertisement appears, though, and to have artwork for your advertisements ready to meet tight deadlines. Nevertheless, substantial discounts can be achieved and you will often be helping out a paper which has had another advertiser cancel at the last minute and suddenly has a blank space to fill.

If an advertising salesperson contacts you, it can be worth making a ridiculously low offer to see what happens. You have to be prepared to lose the space, but it will certainly test how desperate the magazine is to obtain some cash. Sometimes, your offer will be accepted, making you the winner.

Note the style of the letter, which is designed to catch the advertiser off guard: "I have to be completely honest and say that there is no way we can pay your rate-card price...". The argument that "...we have almost exhausted our advertising budget..." tantalisingly suggests that there is some money available, which any company offering advertising is likely to chase. Laying your cards on the table about the amount available to spend is sufficient bait to tempt those who are interested.

BELLS OF BASILDON

Bells of Basildon Ltd, Unit 12, Way Park, Basildon SS12 6DE
Tel: 01268 109 9954 Fax: 01268 109 5576 Reg. No. England 13078453 VAT No: 75698764

Mr R Turner
Readers' Journal
Napier Close
London
N76 5TG

14th October 1999

Dear Roger

Advertising in Readers' Journal
Thank you for contacting me about the availability of advertising space in your journal.

I have to be completely honest and say that there is no way we can pay your rate-card price of £2500. All our off-the-page advertising has to be justified by the number of responses that we are able to generate, and our past experience of your journal is that the responses are not as high as from other media. Coupled with the fact that we have almost exhausted our advertising budget for this year, my instinctive reaction is to say 'no'.

However, we do have just £250 available, which we are willing to spend. If this is of interest, let me know.

Yours sincerely

Paula Little
Advertising Manager

CHAPTER SIX

Banking and Property

This chapter focuses on letters that are ancillary to many core business activities but which are no less important to the smooth running of a business. It deals specifically with letters to the bank and to surveyors.

Banking letters
Among the routine letters to a bank are some notable ones (letters 93–4), which show the kind of information that banks like to see when they ask to be put in the picture about the financial situation.

Property
When purchasing property you will need to arrange for surveys to be done. Letters 95–6 show how to instruct a surveyor.

Occasionally, cheques will go astray or get lost in the post. If this happens, you should cancel the cheque by telephone and confirm it in writing. This will stop anyone else cashing the cheque if it falls into the wrong hands.

Don't forget to give precise details about the cheque (its payee, amount, number and date written).

It will be a help to identify the replacement cheque that has been sent, in case the bank looks for the cheque by amount or otherwise confuses the new cheque with the old.

SIMPSON & MARTIN

39 TOP STREET
STOKE-ON-TRENT
ST2 3DR UNITED KINGDOM
Tel: (01782) 156232 Fax: (01782) 120899
Reg. No: England 96223978 VAT No: 91210674

J W Cross
Manager
RSH Bank PLC
3 Main Street
Stoke-on-Trent
ST2 3RF

7 May 1999

Dear Mr Cross,

Our cheque no. 107348

I am writing to confirm that we would like to cancel cheque no.107348 (dated 2 April 1999) for £2745.89, which was in favour of John C Smith Ltd. I understand there is a charge for stopping a cheque of £7, which will be debited from our account

As I mentioned on the telephone this morning, it appears to have been lost in the post and we are issuing a replacement cheque (No. 107399).

Please confirm that the cheque has been stopped.

Yours sincerely

John Herbert
Finance Director

Taylor Taylor & Shaw

Benton House, Clifton, Bristol BS16 7LJ
Tel: (0117) 1089254   Fax: (0117) 1089211

Brian Fowler
Branch Manager
RSH Bank PLC
16 Main Street
Clifton
Bristol
BS16 7JJ

15 August 1999

Dear Mr Fowler,

Account number 5497610
With the departure of our accountant, Stanley Pritchard, the two
signatures that will appear on the cheques drawn on account number
5497610 will be mine and that of John Barclay, who is replacing Stanley.
This will take effect from 1 September.

I enclose a sample of John's signature for your file and would be grateful if
you could confirm safe receipt.

Yours sincerely

A W Taylor

Partners: AW Taylor & GS Taylor

If a signatory to a cheque
leaves the company, you
will have to notify the
bank of the changes:
which account is
affected; the name of the
old and new signatory;
the date when the
signature will be
accepted from and an
example of the new
signature for the bank's
reference.

If you visit a bank manager seeking funds for a project, he is very unlikely to commit at the meeting to grant you the funds requested. Instead, he will want to take a day or two to consider your proposal and perhaps put it in front of his credit committee. Note how the company uses the time to go back to the bank with a positive statement, which should help tip the balance in your favour, if the bank is undecided whether to lend the money.

BELLS OF BASILDON

Bells of Basildon Ltd, Unit 12, Way Park, Basildon SS12 6DE
Tel: 01268 109 9954 Fax: 01268 109 5576 Reg. No. England 13078453 VAT No: 75698764

Richard Hobbs
Small Business Manager
Barkers Bank PLC
27 High Street
Basildon
SS12 6DF

30 April 1999

Dear Richard,

Re: Our application for a business loan
Thank you for your time on Tuesday, concerning our application for a business loan. We are pleased that your initial reaction to our plan is positive, and that you feel our proposition is viable. We appreciate that you require a few days to consider the plan in detail.

Since our meeting, I am delighted to report that we have finalised the details of the contract to supply Galestreet supermarket, which gives us a guaranteed monthly cash flow of £20,000 per month, £4000 more than the amount we originally anticipated. We are aiming to sign the contract on Friday 27 May and it would be reassuring to know that the finance will be in place to fund the capital-equipment purchase, which is necessary to accommodate the increased output.

I realise this does not give you a lot of time to consider the plan. Nevertheless, I hope it is sufficient for you to give us a response before we sign the contract.

Yours sincerely

Simon Frost
Managing Director

H J KINGSLEY (NORWICH) LTD

Kingsley House, Morris Street, Norwich NR6 7JM
Tel: (01603) 117097 Fax: (01603) 117099 Reg. No: England 12086215 VAT No: 8793519

Mr Peter Edwards
Barkers Bank plc
14 North Street
Norwich
NR6 6JM

10 April 1999

Dear Mr Edwards

Re: Quarterly Review of HJ Kingsley (Norwich) Ltd
I promised to let you have details of our order book as part of the quarterly review.

I am pleased to say that our current orders are 15 per cent up on the comparable period last year, at just over £250,000. Enquiries for which we have quoted total £850,000. Historically, we convert 73 per cent of quotes to firm orders. Based on those figures, our projected sales turnover for the year, as depicted in the cash flow forecast, of £1.75 million, is a prudent assessment of the company's likely performance for the current financial year.

I hope this provides you with the information that you need. If you require any further information please do not hesitate to ask.

Yours sincerely

Colin North
Managing Director

As part of the management of a business account, banks often want to be kept regularly informed about the financial progress of a company. What they are usually most interested in is the state of the current order book and how that translates into a forecast for the coming months.

This letter focuses on the headline figures (which is all the bank will be interested in at present). You can always submit the evidence to support the figures in subsequent documentation.

Note how the letter keeps its attention on figures – it doesn't try to gloss over the picture with a more general statement. This is the kind of approach which will satisfy a bank. If you do attempt to give a general gloss, the bank will be quick to see through this and may come down heavily on you with some penetrating questions.

If the financial picture is positive, you will not be concerned about giving information to the bank. However, if the picture is less than good, it may be tempting to disguise what is happening in the hope that the situation will improve. But this would be the wrong step to take. It may buy you a temporary reprieve, but what if the picture does not improve? You will end up digging yourself into an even bigger hole.

It is far better to face up to the circumstances and find both a way of managing it and of convincing the bank that your strategy will produce the results that are needed. Note how this letter takes a positive approach, even though the news is not good: "...we do have a strategy in place to manage the decline...which will more than compensate and put us ten per cent ahead of the value of our current order book...".

H J KINGSLEY (NORWICH) LTD
Kingsley House, Morris Street, Norwich NR6 7JM
Tel: (01603) 117097 Fax: (01603) 117099 Reg. No: England 12086215 VAT No: 8793519

Mr Peter Edwards
Barkers Bank plc
14 North Street
Norwich
NR6 6JM

10 September 1999

Dear Mr Edwards

Re: Review of HJ Kingsley (Norwich) Ltd
I promised to let you have details of our current position since our review last month. As I indicated over the 'phone, the situation has not improved, but, we do have a strategy in place to manage the decline.

Our current orders are, frankly, disappointing. As at last night the figure was £203,000 which is 4 per cent down on the same period last year. As a consequence, we have trimmed our expenditure by 6 per cent and conducted a detailed analysis of what our customers require. This has produced the evidence that their tastes are moving from the need for a low-cost functional product to a middle-of-the-range quality item. We have redesigned both the product and the packaging to reflect this changing taste, and we plan to have it on the shelves by the end of this year. Although we forecast a fall in the volume of orders, the profitability per item will increase, which will more than compensate and put us ten per cent ahead of the value of our current order book within the next six months.

I hope this strategy meets with your approval and we shall be able to maintain our overdraft at current levels.

Yours sincerely

Colin North
Director

Thomas King & Palmer Ltd

serving the world

24 Fuller Road, Welling,
Kent DA16 7JP
Tel : (01322) 100132
Fax : (01322) 100178

Reg. No : England 1212298762
VAT No : 92905643

Mr J R Holt
W B Webster & Son
6 High Street
Dartford
Kent
DA1 2OB

14 July 1999

Dear Mr Holt,

12a High Street, Welling
Further to our telephone conversation today, I enclose, as requested,
the estate agent's particulars regarding the above property.

I would be grateful if you could give me a quotation for carrying out a
full structural survey on the property and how soon you would be able
to make your inspection.

We have made an offer on the property, although we are waiting to
hear whether it has been accepted.

Yours sincerely

F G York
Director

Before instructing a surveyor to inspect a property, ask him for a quotation for carrying out the work. He will want to know some basic information about the property and what its value is. It may be best to send him the estate agent's details, so he can see how large the property is and how much work is involved. He will usually also want to know the age of the property, which may have a bearing on the amount of work.

If you notice specific defects in a property that require remedial work, when instructing a surveyor to inspect a property, it is worth asking him to make a specific comment on the nature and extent of those defects. You may obtain more detailed advice and a more thorough inspection of the faults, even though you would expect them to be covered in the surveyor's report, together with additional points which you had not noticed. Note the confirmation of the quotation, to prevent any misunderstanding about its cost.

Thomas King & Palmer Ltd

serving the world

24 Fuller Road, Welling,
Kent DA16 7JP
Tel : (01322) 100132
Fax : (01322) 100178

Reg. No : England 1212298762
VAT No : 92905643

Mr J R Holt
W B Webster & Son
6 Bishops Croft
Dartford
Kent
DA1 2OB

14 July 1999

Dear Mr Holt,

12a High Street, Welling

Just to let you know that our offer to purchase the above freehold property for £76,000 has now been accepted and, as I mentioned on the 'phone the other day, I would be grateful if you could carry out a full structural survey. A copy of the estate agent's particulars is enclosed. I understand the fully inclusive cost of the survey will be £327.

I am a little concerned about some of the defects to the property. I am sure that you will pick them up anyway but I thought I should mention them. The small office at the back of the property seems to have an excessively damp smell. I gather it has not been used for some time but I would appreciate if you could investigate any repairs that may be necessary. Also, water appears at some time to have come through into the upstairs front office, next to the chimney breast. Is this a current problem or does it appear as if repairs have been carried out but redecoration has not been done?

I look forward to receiving your report.

Yours sincerely

F G York
Director

CHAPTER SEVEN

Business and the Community

All businesses will, to some extent, have dealings with the community in which they are involved. The letters in this chapter (91–101) deal with requests for charitable donations, an invitation to present an award, handling a request to serve on a local committee and dealing with local residents on planning issues.

Requests and invitations

Handling requests from charities for donations that you are going to accept is easier than declining requests. You have to counter the impression of being mean-minded and uncharitable and finding a good reason is not always easy. The letters here (97–9) show how to approach such requests and the right words to choose if you want to decline.

Handling objections

Letter 101 shows how to react to a controversial development and what to do if you find yourself in the hot-seat, up against some potentially angry local residents. It has some good phrases which will help mollify the objections.

Supporting a charity venture can be good for developing relations with the local community. If you consider helping in this way, with a little thought and planning you may be able to use the opportunity to get the press involved and turn it into a PR opportunity, both for your company and the charity.

Hart & Tucker Ltd

19 Green Street, Maidstone, Kent ME41 1TJ
Telephone: (01622) 109109
Facsimile: (01622) 108106
Reg. No: England 96223978   VAT No: 91210674

Martin Foster
Kids in the Sun
34 Barton Close
Maidstone
Kent
ME41 1JK

16 June 1999

Dear Mrs Foster

Thank you for your letter of 15 June, telling us about your plans to give disabled children the chance to go on holiday.

I think the work that you are doing in this area is tremendous and we would be delighted to donate £2500 towards the cause. In return, I wonder if it might be possible to arrange for a small handing-over ceremony of the cheque with a photographer and perhaps with some of the children who will benefit? We enjoy very good relations with the local press and I believe a photo in the paper would present a excellent opportunity to promote both our causes.

Please let me know what you think about this idea and all the very best of luck in achieving your target of £20,000.

Yours sincerely

Helen Jones
Director

RPP Holdings Plc
35/38 New Road, Paignton, Devon TQ3 4UU
Tel: 01803 175653 Fax: 01803 187908
Reg. No: England 1976143

Mrs Ann Connor
Chairman
Chamber of Commerce
The Town Hall
Clarke St
Paignton
TQ3 4UN

8 May 1999

Dear Ms Connor,

This week we have been awarded registration to ISO 9001, the standard which gives our customers quality guarantees. Obtaining registration to ISO 9001 is a major achievement for our company. It has taken over two years to implement our Quality Management System, something to which the entire workforce of fifty has contributed. It is also a source of great pride that we are the first binder manufacturer in the country to be granted ISO 9001 registration.

To mark the occasion, we are planning to hold a short award ceremony, and I am writing to ask if you would be willing to present the award to us at this unique event. The ceremony will be held at 11.45 am on 15 July, at our premises. The ceremony will be followed by a luncheon.

It will be a tremendous honour for us if you are able to accept this invitation and I look forward to hearing from you.

Yours sincerely

John Herbert
Director

When persuading someone to attend a ceremony, keep the letter as brief as possible. Give the reader sufficient information to understand what the ceremony is for, enough background about the award and when the ceremony will be, but make sure the information is kept relevant and concise. A little bit of flattery will go a long way, as here: "It will be a tremendous honour...".

The charity will be able to appreciate the reason for declining here because the company has a pre-existing policy towards donations and is keen to make "...a more significant contribution...". The tone is formal but polite: "For this reason, I regret we must decline your invitation...".

Offering to have a collecting tin will help take some of the disappointment out of not receiving a corporate donation and make the reader feel that it was worthwhile writing the letter.

Fenner & Sons

16 George Street, Woodbridge,
Suffolk IP3 7KL
Tel: (01394) 198423
Fax: (01394) 198444
Registered in England: 91221299
VAT No: 919129075 80

Mr Paul Middleton
H.D.S.C.F
14 Franklin Gardens
Mildenhall
Suffolk
IP28 7JU

30 July 1999

Dear Mr Middleton,

Your letter of 13 July to John Yippley has been passed to me to reply.

Each year, one per cent of our revenue is allocated to charitable ventures. Last year, we took the decision to commit ourselves to five causes for the next three years. That way, we felt we would be able to make a more significant contribution than if our donations were spread more thinly across many causes. For this reason, I regret we must decline your invitation, but I would like to wish you every success in raising funds for your cause.

If it would be of any help, we would be prepared to keep a collecting tin at our reception so that we may collect donations both from members of staff and visitors to our site. Please let me know if this is of interest.

Yours sincerely

J P Turner
Director

PARKER

Glass Ltd

Unit 27 Willow Park
Christchurch, Dorset BH23 6MM
Tel: 01202 109111
Fax: 01202 109112

Reg. No: England 962578762
VAT No: 9120564

David Firth
Christchurch Business Club
19 Buttercup Gardens
Christchurch
Dorset
BH23 5MM

18 July 1999

Dear David,

Thank you for your letter of 15 July, asking if I would like to sit on the committee representing the interests of the members of the local business club.

I have enjoyed membership of the club, however, my business commitments for the foreseeable future preclude me from taking on any additional outside responsibilities.

I am sorry that I am unable to assist on this occasion and hope you are successful in finding an alternative member who is able to help.

Yours sincerely

Roger Crabb
Marketing Director

This is another potentially tricky letter, but it is better to turn the idea down than to half-heartedly carry out the responsibilities that any committee post inevitably calls for.

The reply here is fairly vague but seems genuine, so is unlikely to provoke a counter-request. Note the use of the phrase "...additional outside responsibilities", suggesting that your obligations are not simply "...business commitments'...".

A letter to a wider local community on a controversial topic needs careful thought before being sent. Feelings could be running high and you may have to work hard to make residents appreciate that their interests have been taken into account and not ignored.

Note the way the letter empathises with the reader from the start: "As residents ourselves, we all understand the depth of feeling...". And note the frank way this letter ends: inviting people to pick up the 'phone helps to portray a picture of honesty and openness that is disarming.

IDENDEN INDUSTRIES
A division of Idenden Plc
Porter House, Hull HU7 4RF England

Tel 01482 119087 Fax 01482 119088
Registered in England No: 1218943

13 April 1999

Dear Resident,

I am writing to you all directly concerning the plans for the quarry at the end of Stone Road in your village. As residents ourselves, we all understand the depth of feeling about this development. We are as concerned as you to ensure that the character of Littlegreen village is not damaged and I would like to reassure you of our commitment to this.

I know you are concerned about the increase in lorry traffic that this development may cause. In our consultation with the local planning authorities, we have given a commitment that all lorries will use a designated route, to minimise the impact caused and to keep the environment as safe as possible for residents. The lorries will travel only between Stone Road and the A113. They will therefore avoid the heart of the village and, apart from the houses on Stone Road, none of the residential areas will be affected. The lorries will be strictly limited in the hours at which they can be driven, to between 7.30am and 7.30pm. Night-time traffic and noise will therefore be avoided.

It is anticipated that the quarry will have a working life of around ten years. As part of the planning agreement, we are committed to returning the quarry to a natural environment when it ceases to have any further commercial use. Indeed, we believe that the plans in hand for a wildlife and waterfowl reserve will enhance the environment tremendously, particularly in an area that has few wetland habitats of this type.

I hope this letter clarifies for many of you the principal issues of concern to you. However, if any of you have any other concerns about the development that you would like to discuss, please pick up the 'phone and call me on the above number, or write to me at the address given.

Yours sincerely

Peter Hand
Director

301 ways to start your letter

As discussed ... requested ... agreed ...

As discussed, will you please send ...

As discussed, I enclose samples of ...

As discussed, I am very sorry for the delay in sending you ...

As requested, I enclose ...

As we agreed this morning, I would like to confirm our mutual decision ...

At our last meeting, it was agreed that ...

As you are aware ...

As I am sure you are aware, ...

As I have previously explained to you, ...

As you are aware, under our holiday policy, the company reserves the right ...

As you are no doubt aware, there are certain confidential and personal files ...

As you are no doubt aware, the recent events in ...

As you know, we deal with a number of different suppliers ...

As you know, we have been working ...

Congratulations ...

Congratulations.

Congratulations on winning ...

Firstly, Mary, I would like to say how delighted I am for you at your news ...

Many congratulations on the birth of your son.

May I be the first to offer you our congratulations on ...

I was delighted to hear you have won ...

I would like to offer you my personal congratulations ...

I am sorry ...

Firstly, apologies for the delay in replying to your fax, which was caused by ...

First of all, my sincere apologies for not responding to your enquiries ...

Firstly, I would like to say how sorry we are that you have had to wait so long ...

I am sorry if this messes you around but our client has just notified us that ...
I am sorry that you feel that you have not received the level of service expected.
I am sorry that you feel the price of ...
I am sorry to hear that you are unable to trace ...
I am sorry to learn of your recent bereavement.
I am very sorry that you were left waiting ...
I am very sorry to hear that you are still not making a good enough recovery ...
I am very sorry.
What can I say? Sorry.
Oops! We've made a real clanger.
We were all very saddened to learn about the sudden death of your wife ...
We were deeply shocked by John's untimely death ...
We were shocked and saddened to hear of Howard Green's fatal accident.
I was very sorry to hear your sad news.
I write as one of Howard's new customers to say how very, very sad we were ...

Following ...

Following our conversation this morning, I am delighted to confirm our offer ...
Following our telephone conversation ...
Following the recent accident involving ...
Following the staff meeting this morning, I am writing to confirm that ...
Following your claim for ...

Further to ...

Further to our recent discussion, I have pleasure in enclosing ...
Further to our recent telephone conversation, I have pleasure in enclosing ...
Further to our telephone conversation, I am writing to introduce you to our ...
Further to your fax this morning: at the moment I am feeling very let down by your ...
Further to your recent conversation with ...
Further to your request for ...

I ...

I note from my diary that you have an appointment to see me on ...
I promised to let you have details of ...
I realise that I should not have ...
I recently saw details of your company's range of ...
I telephoned your office last week for a revised quotation ...
I think it was very useful to talk through your performance over the last six months ...
I don't dispute that other customers have accepted ...
I wrote to you on the 16th September chasing the above order for ...

I am surprised ... disappointed ...

Bob, you personally gave me your word and I trusted you to pay promptly ...
I am surprised to have had no response to my fax dated ...
I am surprised to have received no reply to our previous letter ...
I am afraid that our Financial Director has put these orders on hold ...
I am at a loss to understand why you have not paid us the monies which you owe.
I am extremely disappointed that I find myself having to write to you yet again.
I am now getting very concerned that we have heard nothing from you ...
I am very disappointed that you have not remitted the sum of ...
I am very disappointed with you.
I hoped that I would not have to write to you about ...
I have now sent you a number of fax messages and am disappointed ...
We regret to note that you have failed to respond to our previous reminders ...

I am pleased ...

I am pleased to confirm your appointment as agent for ...
I am pleased to inform you that the company agrees to ...
I am pleased to quote you ex-works prices for the items, as requested.
I am delighted to confirm that you are this year's winner of ...
I am delighted to report that we have had an excellent year ...
I am delighted to say that our sales are ahead of expectations ...
It was a pleasure to meet you and Richard in February ...
It was a pleasure to meet you yesterday, ...
It was great to meet you and your team last week.

I have received ...

I have received a consignment of ...
I have received in the post this morning your invoice no. ...
I have received your catalogue of ...
I am in receipt of your fax of 10 February.
I am in receipt of your letter of 30 June, asking for a reference for ...
I received a copy of your autumn catalogue, giving details of ...
I received, this morning, your invoice no. ...
Yesterday, we received ...
We received your delivery of ...
We today received from you ...
We have received an application from ...

I am writing ...

I am writing concerning your request for a refund ...
I am writing on a matter that is causing ...
I am writing to advise you of a change in our terms and conditions ...
I am writing to clarify the position about the ...

I am writing to confirm our telephone conversation, regarding ...
I am writing to express my growing dissatisfaction of the service we are receiving ...
I am writing to let you know that we have decided not to renew your contract ...
I am writing to thank you for recommending me to ...
I am writing to you because I want you to know of our experience ...
I am responding to the idea that you put forward ...

I confirm ...

I confirm our faxed quotation for ...
I confirm our quote of ...
I confirm that, as of today, we are amending your terms of contract ...
I confirm the points we discussed at our meeting on ...
Just a note to confirm our conversation today ...
Just a quick note to confirm the deal agreed ...
I would just like to confirm that we have considered your request to ...
I write to confirm our order for ...
Confirming my telephone call and your return fax, ...
This is to confirm our meeting at your offices at 10.30am tomorrow, 25 January.
This is to confirm the details and the key terms of the offer we have accepted ...

I enclose ...

I enclose, herewith, a draft copy of ...
I enclose our purchase order for ...
Please find enclosed our cheque to the value of ...
Please find enclosed our statement as at 31 July for £2903.86.

It is ...

It is not often I receive such an abusive letter. In spite of your rude tone ...
It is with a tinge of sadness that I have to announce ...
It is with regret that I tender my resignation as ...
It has come to my attention that you ...
It was useful to review your progress to date ...

I have ...

I have been advised by ...
I have been given your name by ...
I have checked my records and realise that ...
I have considered your letter of 21st January and your assertion that ...
I have just been reviewing ...
I have just come across a product that is so good ...
I have just received your ...
I have just returned from a visit to ...
I have now reviewed your proposal to ...

I hope ...

I hope the last order we supplied to you was satisfactory and met your expectations.
I hope you and Joshua are well and that you are not having too many sleepless nights.

I refer to ...

I refer to our order dated ...
I refer to our order for ...
I refer to our telephone conversation this morning.
I refer to your letter of 11 February.
I refer to your letter of 23rd April 1999 about a consignment of ...

I trust ...

I trust that you enjoyed your break.
I trust that you received our consignment ...
I trust that you have received my previous correspondence.

I understand ...

I understand from my colleague, ...
I understand from our Mr Davies that you are considering moving ...
I understand that, to obtain the price that is right for us, you have asked us to take ...
I understand that you are concerned about the amount of time you have been given ...
We understand that ...

I was appalled ... astonished ... concerned ...

I was appalled to learn that our consignment had not arrived on time with you.
I was astonished when I telephoned your accounts department this morning ...
I was extremely concerned to hear that you have not received ...
I was most disturbed to receive your letter of 20 April, informing me of ...
I was very disturbed to receive your letter, concerning ...
I was given your verbal assurances on Tuesday that you would have no problem ...

I would like to ...

I would like to correct a factual error in your ...
I would like to place a firm order for ...
I would like to remind you of our agreement ...
I would like to tackle a problem that we have come across, ...

Many thanks for ...

Many thanks for agreeing to act as our ...
Many thanks for the cheque for £...., received this morning.
Many thanks for the letters received from both John and yourself, concerning ...

Many thanks for your enquiry for ...
Many thanks for your excellent talk, which ...
Many thanks for your latest offerings.
Many thanks for your letter, asking if we are prepared to offer ...
Many thanks for your letter of 13th January.
Many thanks for your order, received today.

Please ...

Please arrange for the consignment of ...
Please let me have a price on Tuesday 4 April for ...
Please find enclosed our cheque to the value of ...
Please find enclosed our statement as at 31 July for £2903.86.
Please find attached our order for ...
Please find our cheque to the value of £1123.60 to cover our order ...
Please supply a quotation for the following: ....
Please supply and deliver as follows: ...

Thanks for ...

Thanks for coming in to see me last week.
Thanks for coming to put the ...
Thanks for looking into the possibility of arranging ...
Thanks for sending through the latest price changes.
Thanks for your delivery of ...
Thanks for your quotation for ...
Thanks for your fax of 9th May. Sorry that I have sat on it for so long ...

Thank you ....

I felt I had to write to you to say how delighted I have been with ...
Just a note to say thank you for the cheque.
Just a quick note to thank you very much for your time the other day ...
Thank you for allowing me time to assess the above product.
Thank you for applying for a Credit Account with us.
Thank you for asking if we would be interested in buying ...
Thank you for attending the interview last week for the post of ...
Thank you for being so frank and open about the difficulties that you have ...
Thank you for bringing the lower than expected performance to my attention.
Thank you for buying ...
Thank you for coming to see me last ...
Thank you for contacting me about ...
Thank you for letting me know about ...
Thank you for returning the ...
Thank you for sending ... ...
Thank you for taking the trouble to clarify the situation for me.

Thank you for the business which you have brought to us.
Thank you for the courtesy extended to me during my visit to ...
Thank you for your application for a credit account.
Thank you very much indeed for your extremely pleasant letter ...
Thank you very much for arranging a most enjoyable day for me.

Thank you for your ...

Thank you for your application for the post of ...
Thank you for your cheque for £1500 in part settlement of your account.
Thank you for your comments on our proposed discount.
Thank you for your completed application form for the position of ...
Thank you for your enquiry about the price of ...
Thank you for your fax, which I received this morning, asking if ...
Thank you for your fax, regarding payment for your orders.
Thank you for your invoice no. ...
Thank you for your kind invitation to ...
Thank you for your latest delivery, received today
Thank you for your letter dated 17th February, addressed to our Managing Director,
   which has been brought to my attention.
Thank you for your letter dated 9th September, addressed to our Managing Director,
   who has passed this to me for my attention.
Thank you for your letter expressing concern about the service you are receiving ...
Thank you for your letter of 11th September and for the samples ...
Thank you for your letter of 12 June, concerning the carriage charge on our invoice.
Thank you for your letter of 12 June, outlining the terms ...
Thank you for your letter of 15 July, notifying us that ...
Thank you for your letter of 20 June, regarding ...
Thank you for your letter of 21 May, advising us ...
Thank you for your letter of 24 June, applying for the post of ...
Thank you for your letter of 26 January, asking about the terms for ...
Thank you for your letter of 3 June, enquiring if we have any vacancies for ...
Thank you for your letter of 30 April in response to our order ...
Thank you for your letter of 3rd December and for your kind comments.
Thank you for your letter of 7th March, which reached me today.
Thank you for your letter of the 5th July, expressing concern over ...
Thank you for your letter, querying the price of ...
Thank you for your order against our quotation no. ...
Thank you for your payment of £..., which, I note, was credited to our account ...
Thank you for your prices, received this morning.
Thank you for your proposed price ...
Thank you for your recent enquiry.
Thank you for your recent faxes. I apologise for the delay in replying.
Thank you for your recent order for the enclosed ...
Thank you for your recent order. I am afraid that we have temporarily sold out of ...

Thank you for your recent telephone call, regarding ...
Thank you for your request for a reference for ...
Thank you for your suggestion that we ...
Thank you for your telephone call today.
Thank you for your time on Tuesday, concerning ...
Thank you very much for your letter about ...

We...

We are a small company, specialising in ...
We are currently seeking to be registered ...
We are in receipt of your cheque for ...
We are intending to trade with ...
We are interested in ...
We are pleased to announce the appointment of ...
We are reorganising the administration of our accounts department ...
We have an outstanding debt of ...
We have been notified by ...
We have considered your request to operate an agency ...
We have decided to change the holiday policy of the company.
We have just learned about the death of ...
We have just secured an unexpectedly large order ...
We have noticed some abuses of the telephone for private calls ...
We have recently received the enclosed Statement from you.
We have reviewed the price changes to our products for the next 12 months.
We have supplied you with items on four separate occasions to the value of ...
We met at the Multimedia 99 show (on the Wednesday) and you showed me ...
We no longer need ...
We note that you have failed to respond to our previous demands to settle ...
We wish to obtain ...
We would like to carry out some amendments to ...

With reference to ...

With reference to our recent telephone conversation, ...
With reference to our telephone conversation, I have pleasure in introducing ...
With reference to the above, we have received ...
With regard to the above, we enclose ...
Re: your fax to our accounts manager of ...
Re: your recommendation of ...

You ...

You have been issued with ...
You have been specially selected to receive one of our star prizes ...
You have received two written warnings about ...

You may have heard rumours circulating ...
You supplied us with a new ...

Your ...

Your account has been passed to me for attention ...
Your account with us is now SERIOUSLY OVERDUE.
Your company has opened a credit account with us.
Your customer ... has applied to us for a credit account ...
Your subscription to ... will be expiring within the next three months.

More notes to start on ...

A week ago, you arranged for ...
According to my records, you still owe ...
As a company committed to providing a quality service, ...
As you are a valued customer, we want every pound you spend with us to save you
    money.
Having arrived back safely ...
Here is our ...
In April this year, you ordered ...
In case you failed to receive the details we sent last month of our fabulous ...
In conversation with your colleague, Mary, yesterday, it emerged that ...
In response to your telephone enquiry this morning, I am writing to announce that ...
Just a quick note to let you know that ...
On 30 September, we placed an order for ...
On 6 August, we received from you a consignment of ...
On a recent visit to your company, I left our company brochure for your attention ...
Our agreement of 20 January stipulates that you undertake to supply us with ...
Payment for this order was due in ...
The response to our advertisement for an Office Manager has exceeded ...
Since we have acquired ...
Something very peculiar appears to have been happening with ...
Until now, it has been a requirement of the company that everyone ...
With the departure of ...

201 nice turns of phrase

With so many power-packed phrases tucked away in the letters, it can be difficult to find the right one at the right time. This appendix aims to overcome this problem by distilling a selection of over 200 of the best phrases for you to choose from. It concentrates on phrases with mood and emotion so, whether you are having to write a letter of condolence, persuade someone to your way of thinking or bring a supplier up sharply, you are certain to find the right phrase to fit the moment.

Stern phrases

I trust our purchase order instructions will be rigidly adhered to in future.

As they have not been received by the due date, we are exercising our right under the agreement to cancel the order forthwith.

I was surprised to see a carriage charge included for ...

No mention was made of this charge ...

Our purchase order referred expressly to the fact that delivery was to be included in the price ...

You may recall that when I placed the order, you granted us a special discount ...

... it should be little more than an extension of what your current practices are ...

We expect our suppliers to give us the service that we demand ...

It will certainly make us think twice about using you in the future ...

Unless you can agree to do our printing profitably within the price agreed, we will probably have to agree to part company.

I expect a full refund by return.

We shall have no option but to seek an alternative supplier.

I am therefore bound to advise you that ...

Please give it your most urgent attention.

It is time this matter was brought to a close.

... we shall not hesitate in disallowing the commission payment ...

... it is naturally disconcerting ...

It is also particularly disappointing ...

You have not had the authority ...

I was led to believe that this was included in your quotation

... your failure to notify us ...

Your conduct in this matter has been extremely disappointing ...

I was very disturbed ...

... we have already had to make several representations ...

We object in the strongest terms ...

I hope this makes our position clear ...

We expect you to accomplish it within the agreed deadline and budget.

We must have a solution if you are to retain our custom.

I regard this behaviour as totally unprofessional.

I am not satisfied that the goods are of merchantable quality.

Since the goods are not fit for the purpose intended ...

I must stress that, in placing this order with you, ...

... it was absolutely conditional on your ability to meet our deadline.

... for which we shall seek compensation.

I was astounded to find that ...

... we shall be seeking recompense for any losses that we incur.

... the occasion was a shambolic disaster from start to finish.

I strongly sense that you are taking us for granted ...

... the entire job is simply unacceptable...

I am particularly irritated that, once again, you are blaming ...

I am hoping that you will take these issues more seriously than your colleagues appear
   to ...

Contractual phrases

Under the terms of our agreement ...

... I trust that you will abide by the terms of our agreement.

I would like to draw your attention to the agreement...

Our agreement expressly forbids you ...

... in full and final settlement ...

... it was a condition of our contract ...

As you have not kept to the terms of your contract ...

... failure to comply with our terms ...

... we shall have no option but to terminate ...

... we are exercising our right not to pay ...

... we undertake to rectify ...

... we have made good the defect ...

... we have honoured our contract to you ...

... we shall have no option but to terminate ...

Letting someone down lightly

At the moment, it does not fit in comfortably with our plans for the immediate future ...

I am afraid I must say "Thanks, but no thanks".
Our decision was arrived at after a great deal of discussion and thought.
It was not an easy decision to make ...
While I believe that your experience is right for us, ...
I am confident that you would be able to secure a good number of orders for our business but ...
... it would not be fair to either of us ...

Phrases that trigger people's emotional responses

You will understand that, as a business, we put a high premium on reliability.
I am feeling very let down by your company ...
... don't have a moral leg to stand upon ...
... really should know better ...
It was not we who caused this problem ...

Phrases that charm customers

... as a special favour ...
... enclosed is the guarantee which sets out our promises and your rights ...
We look forward to a long and happy association with your business.
Should we fall short of your high expectations in any matter ...
... please contact me personally.
... and trust that this helps in compensating you for your dissatisfaction.
We are, of course, concerned to offer you the best possible service ...
... as you are a highly valued customer ...
Anticipating that this arrangement will be acceptable to you, I have pleasure in enclosing ...
... you have been specially chosen ...
... we are asking a select group of our customers ...
... you will avoid immeasurable hassle ...

Making a gentle request

... we will have to ask you ...
... I do not consider it unreasonable to ask you to ...
I don't want to put you to any trouble, but it would be enormously helpful ...
I appreciate this is a busy time for you, but I wonder if ...
It therefore does not seem unreasonable to request ...

Phrases that aim to reassure

I confirm that we are happy to stand by our original quotation.
I assure you it is perfectly normal and will not impede its function.
... it does not fulfil the high standard that we demand and you, as a customer, expect.
... would not dream of stepping beyond the powers ...

123

I am appalled at how you have been treated ...
I was most disturbed to receive your letter ...
... the intention is not to squeeze a quart out of a pint pot.
... before you come running to us crying 'foul' ...
I know how frustrating it is to be left high and dry ...
I trust everything is in order ...

Making sincere apologies

If I could perhaps explain the circumstances that occurred, not as an excuse, but so
   you can see the exceptional and unexpected difficulties that we faced.
I am deeply sorry that we have let you and your client down ...
This unfortunate event has highlighted a gap in our procedures.
I am extremely sorry this has occurred ...
This is a very rare occurrence (it happens about once a year) ...
Please accept our unreserved apologies.
I have made enquiries and have discovered that in this instance one of our internal
   procedural systems failed.
I do hope that this will go some way to restoring your faith in us.
It seems you have been plagued by gremlins on this occasion.
I have pushed you to the front of the waiting list ...
We are all real people in this company, who try very hard indeed to give a fast and
   efficient service.
I am sorry that you feel that you have not received the level of service expected.
I am confident that you should not experience the same level of disruption now.
I am sorry for any inconvenience caused.
I apologise for this oversight ...

Refusing and rejecting

I regret that we are unable to assist you further in this matter.
For this reason, I regret we must decline your kind invitation ...
I am sorry that we cannot be more helpful on this occasion.
Although, as is clear, I do not agree with much of your letter ...
... I very much regret that we must insist ...
While we do not like to impose unnecessary restrictions ...
I regret that we have decided not to take your application further on this occasion.
I have to be completely honest and say that there is no way we can pay ...
... I wish to deny in the strongest terms possible ...
... we refute your claim.
... I cannot think of any circumstance in which I would dream of agreeing ...
I do not accept your assertions ...

Persuasive phrases

... the charge reflects a contribution only towards the final cost ...

... we do everything we can to keep the charges as competitive as possible ...

... all our suppliers accept it, without exception ...

... we shall have no option but to seek an alternative supplier.

... I guarantee that you will experience the best ...

... we have striven to keep the price increases to an absolute minimum ...

... we see this as a modest contribution towards our continued mutual success ...

... it would not be in our best interests ...

... we are taking on the chin the cost of inflation and the increased cost of ...

Chasing payment

We have now decided to take legal advice on this matter, with a view to the recovery of our money ...

... instructions will be issued to our solicitors to proceed against you.

... please arrange immediate settlement.

... this thorny issue of payment ...

... remit this by return ...

... in view of the one-sided nature of our correspondence ...

... the matter will be passed into other hands in seven days.

... I hope you will render this action unnecessary ...

If you have sent your remittance in the last few days, please disregard this letter.

No further reminders will be issued.

We appreciate this act of good faith ...

... despite our best efforts to obtain payment from you ...

Responding to requests for payment

The reasons for the delay are both tedious and convoluted.

Should any future invoices slip through the net ...

I am extremely embarrassed about the long delay ...

Praise, flattery and recognition

... because you are the best person for the job ...

I will respect your decision, whatever it is.

... thank you personally for all the hard work ...

Thank you once again for your major contribution ...

... the best minds are devoted to this project ...

... I am delighted to announce that you are eligible to receive ...

Congratulations on taking the initiative ...

... I am very impressed by their versatility ...

Your role in this is, of course, pivotal.

... I applaud your enthusiasm for not missing a sale ...

It will be a tremendous honour ...
It gives me great personal pleasure to recognise ...

Threatening to take legal action

While we have no quarrel with your business ...
... we intend to take legal action against ...
... unless she agrees to abide by the terms of our agreement ...
... we shall commence legal proceedings against her.

Warnings

I must warn you ...
... we find it inexcusable ...
... failure to do so ...
You have been given every opportunity ...
As you have chosen to ignore all the warnings ...
... we have no alternative ...
... you must not undertake ...
... you were unable to give us a satisfactory reason ...

Offering help and assistance

... we shall be only too happy to provide ...
We will do everything we can to help ...
... I shall be keeping my fingers crossed.

Motivational

... I know you will be very capable of successfully accomplishing ...
You have a great deal to contribute ...
I am confident that there will be considerable opportunities to increase your
    responsibilities.
I know you will do your utmost ...
I know you will be able to make a major contribution ...
... it is a tribute to your hard work ...
It means a great deal to me, personally, ...

Condolence

We were deeply shocked ...
... it will be very difficult for us to forget ...
We will miss him sorely.
Please accept our sincere sympathy.
We were shocked and saddened ...

126

Selling phrases

... will cut a swathe through the tasks ...
By far the best, ever.
... that makes the guide, for me, utterly irresistible.
... quickly and confidently ...
Do have a look at it ...
... a return that is <u>absolutely guaranteed</u>.
... you do not, absolutely not, have to buy anything from us ...
What do you have to lose?
I have just come across ...
... we felt it essential to let you know about it ...
Just complete the fax-back acceptance offer ... before everyone else does.
... outstanding value for money ...

Appealing for donations

... go a little way to help ...
... find the heart to help ...
... It's not a lot to ask ...

Keeping your options open

Your payment terms are subject to the timing of our payment runs.
However, we reserve the right to return ...

Keeping a supplier firmly *on* the hook

I accept this as a gesture of apology but not as a satisfactory recompense for the late delivery.

Exaggerating a point slightly

It has cost us up to £400 more a month ...

Preparing the ground for bad news

I very much regret that, as from 1st May, we must increase prices of this product ...

185 ways to finish your letter

Best ...

Best regards.
Best wishes.
Best wishes and good luck.
Best wishes from myself and all at ...

I ...

I am grateful that you took the trouble to write ...
I am returning the item with this letter and expect a full refund of ...
I am sorry for any inconvenience caused.
I am sorry that we cannot be more helpful on this occasion.
I do hope that this will go some way to restoring your faith in us.
I enclose a stamped addressed envelope for your convenience when you reply.
I have pleasure in enclosing ...
I have pleasure in returning the product as required ...
I must insist that, from now on, we are given priority treatment.
I regret that we are unable to assist you further in this matter.
I therefore look forward to your immediate reassurance ...
I very much regret that we shall be unable to offer you a refund.

I hope ...

I hope that we continue to be of benefit to you in the future.
I hope they are a success for you.
I hope this arrangement is acceptable to you.
I hope this arrangement is satisfactory.
I hope this explains the position but, if you have any other queries, please do ask.
I hope this information helps you.
I hope this makes our position clear.
I hope this matter can now be closed.
I hope this plan meets with your approval.

I hope this proposal will be of interest to you.
I hope you are willing to help us in this matter.
I hope you have a very successful and prosperous New Year.
I hope you will be able to agree to this proposal.

I look forward to ...

I look forward to a long, fruitful and communicative business relationship.
I look forward to a long and prosperous association with your company.
I look forward to continuing a close relationship with your business in the future.
I look forward to hearing from you and, of course, to receiving your order.
I look forward to hearing from you at your earliest convenience.
I look forward to hearing from you shortly.
I look forward to hearing from you, with regard to ...
I look forward to hearing from you.
I look forward to meeting you all again soon.
I look forward to meeting you.
I look forward to receiving confirmation of your order.
I look forward to receiving your remittances by return.
I look forward to receiving your reply.
I look forward to seeing you again shortly.
I look forward to seeing you on your next visit to the UK.
I look forward to your advice on this matter.
I look forward to your further enquiries.
I look forward to your immediate response.

I trust ...

I trust that further action will now be taken and look forward to your response.
I trust that you find these of interest.
I trust that you will abide by the terms of our agreement.
I trust this gives you the information that you require.
I trust this is a satisfactory summary of our conversation.
I trust this is all in order and hope that you are satisfied with the goods as supplied.
I trust this summarises our conversation satisfactorily.
I trust you will take the above into account.

I would ...

I would appreciate it if you could amend your records accordingly.
I would appreciate it if you could settle the account by the end of this month.
I would be grateful if one of your representatives could telephone me ...
I would be grateful if you could arrange for ....
I would be grateful if you could confirm safe receipt.
I would like to take this opportunity to wish you every success in your future.

If ...

If anyone has any queries about this new policy, please come and see me at any time.
If I can be of any further assistance to you, please do not hesitate to contact me.
If not, please arrange immediate settlement.
If there is anything we can do, please let us know.
If this is of interest, let me know.

If you ...

If you are interested in any of these, do give me a call.
If you are still unable to locate the item, please let me know.
If you do not receive the items by next Tuesday, please let me know.
If you have any further queries on this matter, please contact me again.
If you have any further questions, please do not hesitate to contact me.
If you have any more queries, please do not hesitate to contact me.
If you have any queries, please give me a call.
If you have any queries, please contact me on ...
If you have any questions, or need any further information, please give me a call.
If you have sent your remittance in the last few days, please disregard this letter.
If you need further information, please do not hesitate to contact us.
If you require any further information, please do not hesitate to ask.
If you would like further information, please ring us on ...

In the meantime ...

In the meantime, please could you arrange for ...
In the meantime, I shall ensure that ...
In the meantime, if you have any queries, please give me a ring.

It ...

It is essential that these instructions are adhered to, strictly.
It is time this matter was brought to a close.
It would be appreciated if you could let me know, by return.

Kind ...

Kind regards
Kindest regards.

Let me know ...

Let me know if this is of interest to you.
Let me know if you find out any details and, once again, many thanks for your help.
Let me know what you decide. I will respect your decision, whichever way it goes.
Let me know your thoughts.

Many thanks for ...

Many thanks for your co-operation.

Many thanks for your help.

Many thanks for your prompt and courteous attention to this matter.

Many thanks for your time and effort on our behalf.

Once again, ...

Once again, please accept our sincerest apologies.

Once again, please accept our apologies.

Once again, my sincere apologies.

Once again, thank you very much indeed for taking the trouble to write to me.

Please accept ...

Please accept my apologies for this delay.

Please accept our most sincere condolences and deepest sympathy, from all at ...

Please accept our sincere apologies for the distress caused.

Please accept our sincere apologies for this slight deterioration in service.

Please accept our sincere sympathy for your loss.

Please accept our unreserved apologies.

Please ...

Please advise me of ...

Please call me back urgently, so we can discuss this.

Please cancel ...

Please come back to me if it does not solve the problem.

Please confirm whether this time is convenient for you.

Please arrange for the balance to be supplied as soon as possible.

Please give this matter your most urgent attention.

Please let me know if anything goes wrong again.

Please do not hesitate to call me, should there be any issue that you want to discuss.

Please do not hesitate to contact us, should you need any further information.

Please do not hesitate to get in contact, if we can be of further assistance.

Please find enclosed a copy of our current price list, as requested.

Please give me a call if you would like to set up a meeting.

Please give me a ring if anything is unclear.

Please let me know if this arrangement is of interest.

Please let me know if you think this outline plan is suitable.

Please let me know when these samples will be sent.

Please, please, please supply us with the missing items ASAP.

Please telephone me on receipt of this letter, to let me know ...

Please transfer the remaining balance to account no. ...

Please try to answer these queries quickly, to enable us to ...

Should you ...

Should you be uncertain about any aspect of it, please do not hesitate to give us a call.
Should you have any urgent enquiries, please do not hesitate to contact me personally.
Should you require any further information, please do not hesitate to contact us.

Sorry ...

Sorry for any inconvenience caused by this matter.
Sorry for any trouble caused.

Thank you ...

Thank you again for your assistance, and all good wishes for a successful ...
Thank you for the interest you have shown in our Company.
Thank you for your assistance in this matter.
Thank you for your attention to this matter.
Thank you for your co-operation with this policy.
Thank you for your co-operation in this matter.
Thank you for your help with this matter.
Thank you for your interest in our range of products.
Thank you for your interest.
Thank you for your kind attention.
Thank you for your time and efforts on our behalf.
Thank you in advance for your co-operation.
Thank you, once again, for your kindness.
Thank you once again.
Thank you very much indeed for taking the trouble to write to reassure me.
Thanking you in advance.
Thanking you in anticipation of your assistance in this matter.

We hope ...

We hope never to hear from you again.
We hope you find the package of value and look forward to your future custom.

We look forward ...

We look forward to a long and happy association with your business.
We look forward to hearing from you.
We look forward to helping you save money throughout the coming year.
We look forward to receiving your payment.
We look forward to seeing you then.
We look forward to welcoming you as a customer.
We look forward to your valued, continued support.
We look forward to receiving your cheque by return.

We ...

We regret, therefore, that we must decline your kind offer.

We shall keep you informed, as and when developments occur.

We thank you for this order and look forward to your further enquiries.

We very much appreciate your help in this matter.

We would appreciate your quotation by fax and at the latest by Thursday 12 June.

With ...

With kind regards.

With very best wishes,

Would you ...

Would you kindly acknowledge receipt of this letter and confirm ...

Would you kindly arrange for someone to come and ...

Would you please confirm that ...

Your ...

Your immediate response (and payment) would be appreciated.

Your order will be dispatched as soon as we receive your remittance.

More notes to end on ...

A quick reply would be much appreciated.

Any future orders will have to be paid for in advance.

As stated, we will be having no further dealings with your company.

Do let me know what you decide and I shall be keeping my fingers crossed.

Finally, I enclose the form duly completed and signed.

Give me a call to let me know when you are coming.

Hope to speak to you soon.

Just tick the box on the enclosed reply-paid envelope and send it back to us.

May we take this opportunity of thanking you for your valued support during ...

Regards.

The agenda for this meeting is attached.

This does not help to foster confidence in our business together.

To find out how we can help you, call me now on ...

Whatever the cause of the delay may be, we must have a solution ...

INDEX

Free Special Report

(published price £14.95)

Which one would you like?

- ❏ Dirty Negotiating Tactics and their Solutions
- ❏ Organise Yourself to be Lazy
- ❏ Clear Your Desk Once and For All
- ❏ How to Bankrupt a Rogue Company
- ❏ The Two Minute Presentation Planner
- ❏ Achieving ISO9000 - How much will it cost?
- ❏ Finding and Bidding for Bargain Properties at Auction

We would like to send you the Free Special Report of your choice.

Why?

Because we would like to add your name to our Business Enquirers Group – a selection of business people who receive regular information from us. We will offer you the best and most practical business books published, newsletters, a book review service and also offers from other companies with products and services that may interest you.

To order your free report and join the Business Enquirers Group, simply phone fax or write, give us your name, job title, address, phone, fax and e-mail numbers (if available) and quote MM02. And don't forget to tell us which report you want!

☎ 01353 665544

Ask for your free report by title and remember to quote our reference MM02

Fax 01353 667666

Photocopy this page, complete this box and fax it through to us

```
Name _____  Job title _____
Company _____
Address _____
_____  Post code _____
Phone _____  Fax _____  e-mail _____
```

Post

Wyvern Business Library MM02, FREEPOST CB511, Ely, Cambs CB7 4BR

Photocopy this page, fill in the box above (or staple your business card to it) and send it to us (no stamp required).